OUT OF THE NIGHT
———AND———
INTO THE DREAM

**Contributions to the Study of
Science Fiction and Fantasy**

OUT OF THE NIGHT
——AND——
INTO THE DREAM

*A Thematic Study of the Fiction
of J. G. Ballard*

Gregory Stephenson

Contributions to the Study of Science Fiction and Fantasy, Number 47

Greenwood Press
New York • Westport, Connecticut • London

Library of Congress Cataloging-in-Publication Data

Stephenson, Gregory.
    Out of the night and into the dream : a thematic study of the
fiction of J. G. Ballard / Gregory Stephenson.
        p.   cm.— (Contributions to the study of science fiction and
fantasy, ISSN 0193–6875 ; no. 47)
    Includes bibliographical references and index.
    ISBN 0–313–27922–5 (alk. paper)
    1. Ballard, J. G., 1930–   —Criticism and interpretation.
    2. Science fiction, English—History and criticism.   I. Title.
    II. Series.
    PR6052.A46Z88   1991
    823′.914—dc20   91–21167

British Library Cataloguing in Publication Data is available.

Library of Congress Catalog Card Number: 91–21167
ISBN: 0–313–27922–5
ISSN: 0193–6875

First published in 1991

Greenwood Press, 88 Post Road West, Westport, CT 06881
An imprint of Greenwood Publishing Group, Inc.

Printed in the United States of America

The paper used in this book complies with the
Permanent Paper Standard issued by the National
Information Standards Organization (Z39.48–1984).

10 9 8 7 6 5 4 3 2 1

Copyright Acknowledgment

The author and publisher are grateful to the following for allowing the use of material:
Reprinted from J. G. Ballard, "Which Way to Inner Space?" *New Worlds*, 40 no. 118
(May 1962).

For
William P. Schaefer

Man does not look to the sun in vain; he demands light and warmth not for the corpse which he will one day discard but for his inner being. His greatest desire is to burn with ecstasy, to commerge his little flame with the central fire of the universe. If he accords the angels wings so that they may come to him with messages of peace, harmony and radiance from worlds beyond, it is only to nourish his own dreams of flight, to sustain his own belief that he will one day reach beyond himself, and on wings of gold. . . . The song of creation springs from the ruins of earthly endeavor. The outer man dies away in order to reveal the golden bird which is winging its way toward divinity.

—Henry Miller
The Time of the Assassins

Contents

Introduction

The work of J. G. Ballard represents a sustained act of subversion. It is, moreover, subversion of an ultimate character, directed against nothing so trivial as the governmental or economic systems, but aimed instead at overturning the most fundamental assumptions of our culture regarding the nature of reality and of our own identities. Ballard's writing is, as we shall discover, subversive in the most precise sense of the word—whose original meaning is *to turn from beneath*—in that his fiction upholds the work of forces within the human psyche that are beneath the threshold of conscious awareness, forces that seek to overturn the state of self-conscious selfhood and to overthrow the structure of time and space. And yet these energies which are so inimical to our cherished notions of reality and identity are not malign but benign; their purpose is the redemption of the real and eternal from the false and the finite.

The central concern of Ballard's art is, then, with the problem of exceeding or escaping the limitations of the material world, the space-time continuum, the body, the senses and ordinary ego consciousness, all of which are seen as illusory in nature. In various wise, the themes of transcendence and illusion inform nearly all of the author's work, and have often been misconstrued by critics as representing a nihilistic or fatalistic preoccupation on the part of the author with devolution, decay, dissolution, and entropy.[1] In the following study of Ballard's work, I would like to trace in the author's short fiction and in his novels the development of the themes of transcendence and illusion, together with their concomitant themes, arguing that these themes represent neither an expression of universal pessimism nor a negation of human values and goals, but, rather, an affirmation of the highest humanistic and metaphysical ideal: the repossession for humankind of authentic and absolute being.

In the field of Ballard criticism there are two forerunners to the present study which I want to acknowledge. David Pringle's monograph, *Earth is the Alien Planet* (1979), though dated now in terms of Ballard's subsequent literary production, remains an important study of the author's work and contains many valuable insights.[2] Everyone who has since written on Ballard and every Ballard enthusiast owes a debt of respect and gratitude to this excellent and pioneering work. I learned of Peter Brigg's work, *J. G. Ballard* (1985), only when this present study was completed, but it clearly makes an important contribution to the field.[3] Since the emphases and perspectives of Pringle's and of Brigg's works on Ballard are substantially different from each other and from those of my own study, I believe that our separate works supplement rather than contend with each other.

Before presenting my thematic study of J. G. Ballard's fiction, I want to say something concerning the critical perspectives according to which I have considered the author's work. In essence, my approach to Ballard's work consists of a combination of elements of New Critical methodology with elements of Archetypal criticism. I discuss the individual works of the author in terms of imagery and theme, tracing recurrent motifs and making comparisons among the works, and I also regard the texts in terms of their relationship to myth and archetype, and to the psychic processes that myth and archetype embody. I like to think of my approach as one of first taking a close look at the texture or fabric of the text, and then drawing back for a view from a distance in order to discern the larger design.

My close-reading of the texts will, I think, require no further explanation, but a clarification of certain of the terms and concepts which I have borrowed from the field of Archetypal criticism may prove helpful to the reader and may also serve to suggest something of the larger context of Ballard's writing.

The chief sources of inspiration for my archetypal perspectives upon Ballard's fiction have been the writings of Mircea Eliade, Joseph Campbell, Northrop Frye, and C. G. Jung.

To Eliade, I am chiefly indebted for his discussion of the archetypes of flight and ascension, the paradise myth and the myth of the Fall, together with his descriptions of initiatory ordeals, including those of death and resurrection. Eliade establishes the centrality and universality of the paradise myth and of human striving to return to the paradisiac condition. This striving to exceed time and the limitations of matter and the body—expressed in many different ways throughout human history and among the various cultures of the world, yet fundamentally the same aspiration—Eliade names "the Nostalgia for Paradise," describing it as "the desire to recover the state of freedom and beatitude before 'the Fall,' the will to restore communication between Earth and Heaven; in a word to abolish all the changes made in the very structure of the cosmos and in the human mode of being by that primordial disruption."[4] Such a "Nostalgia for Paradise" and such aspirations and strivings to recover the paradisiac state are, as we shall see, primary characteristics of Ballard's writing.

Eliade further discusses the symbolism of the ancient and universal motifs of flight and ascension as expressive of the human desire to pass beyond the realm of the sensorial and to achieve transcendence and full freedom of being: "to go beyond and 'above' the human condition, . . . to transmute the corporeal modality of man into a spiritual modality."[5] Eliade views such desires as having their roots in the depths of the psyche, and as being absolutely essential and constitutive to the human identity. The motifs of flight and ascension are recurrent throughout Ballard's fiction, and the theme of the human appetite for transcendence as being rooted in the depths of the psyche—in the unconscious mind—is fundamental to the author's work.

From Joseph Campbell's seminal work, *The Hero with a Thousand Faces*, I have taken Campbell's central conception of the monomyth or the journey of the mythic hero, who responding to a call (or unknowingly, involuntarily) embarks upon a quest, undertakes a journey, leaving behind the world of the familiar and entering the realm of the unknown.[6] In the course of his journey the hero undergoes various initiatory ordeals, sometimes including death and resurrection. The hero encounters a tyrannical, merciless male figure with whom he does battle and whom he, at last, slays. And he encounters a female figure to whom he is attracted and whom he beds or marries. In actuality, these figures represent extensions of himself, aspects of his own consciousness. The ultimate effect of the journey and its ordeals upon the hero is that having "died to his personal ego," he arises again, "established in the Self."[7] In various guises the central elements of the hero-journey are prominent in Ballard's oeuvre.

Northrop Frye's discussion of the essential structure of the quest-romance, of the quest-hero's crucial struggle with his antagonist, and of the role of the quest-hero as messianic figure and as redeemer, in his study *Anatomy of Criticism*, also possesses pertinence for the understanding of the protagonists of Ballard's fiction.[8] Frye's treatment of the topic represents a valuable support for and supplement to Joseph Campbell's exposition. Frye points out that "the hero of romance is analogous to the mythical Messiah or deliverer . . . and his enemy is analogous to the demonic powers . . . the opposite poles of the cycles of nature are assimilated to the opposition of the hero and his enemy. The enemy is associated with winter, darkness, confusion, sterility, moribund life, and old age, and the hero with spring, dawn, order, fertility, vigor, and youth."[9] Frye's discussion of what he terms "the flood archetype," which "usually takes the form of some cosmic disaster destroying the whole fictional society," also bears an obvious relevance to Ballard's writing in which disaster and apocalypse are recurrent motifs.[10]

Of particular value as a perspective upon Ballard's writing are certain of the essential tenets of Jungian psychology, including the concepts of a collective unconscious, the process of individuation, and the characterization of the shadow and the anima/animus archetypes. There are significant affinities between these elements of Jungian psychology and particular motifs and themes in the work of J. G. Ballard.

According to Jungian psychology, the process of individuation consists of the growth and evolution of the psyche from "ego" to "Self," that is to say the development of consciousness from an ego-centered identity, that of the conscious personality, to the realization of the inner-center, the unconscious nucleus of identity, the latent totality of the psyche. The process of individuation is motivated by the power of the Self, by its urge to realize itself and to manifest its identity. Working in accordance with its own "secret design," the "supra-personal force" of the Self actively interferes with and opposes the conscious purposes and aims of the ego-identity.[11] Key phases of the individuation process involve encounters on the part of the external, ego-personality with personified aspects of the unconscious, figures which Jung has named the shadow and the anima.

The shadow is defined as "the primitive, uncontrolled and animal part of ourselves," the embodiment of our egotistical attitudes and infantile appetites.[12] It is the dark side of our consciousness, compounded of our self-seeking motives, our vanity and ambition, our attraction to violence and power. At the same time, the shadow contains certain valuable qualities which must be redeemed, refined. The shadow manifests itself as "a person of the same sex" as our own.[13] The confrontation with this aspect of our psyche is a necessary phase of self-recognition, and the struggle with the shadow, the contest to subdue and to convert its energies and to redeem its positive qualities, is an essential step in the process of individuation.

The anima or animus figure (anima for males, animus for females) is the personification of the unconscious in the form of a figure of the sex opposite our own. This figure is even more ambiguous than the shadow, possessing both beneficent and baleful aspects, depending upon whether it has been recognized, honored, and cultivated or disregarded, neglected, and repressed. Thus it may assume the guise of the *femme fatale* or *homme fatale*, or, more frequently, it may serve to open "the way into more profound inner depths," assuming the role of "guide or mediator to the world within and to the Self."[14]

The goal of individuation is the integration, liberation and transformation of consciousness, the realization of the Self. Anima and shadow figures are, as we shall see, prominent in Ballard's fiction, and his work is informed by his own personal version of the process of individuation, a process of psychic evolution that the author depicts as occurring both on an individual level and on a collective human level.

The concepts and perspectives of Mircea Eliade, Joseph Campbell, Northrop Frye, and C. G. Jung reinforce and supplement each other in a number of ways, and from their areas of contact, continuity, and affinity I have formed the synthesis that constitutes the more theoretical aspect of my critical approach in this study. I would like to emphasize, though, that an archetypal approach to Ballard's fiction was suggested to me by my encounter with the author's works themselves. I did not conceive of it a priori and then attempt to impose it grid-like upon the works, but rather it was through reading Ballard's stories and novels that I was inspired to undertake such an approach.

There are two additional sources that should be named and cited. Though these sources are outside of the area of Archetypal criticism, they have served to impart inspiration and direction to my study of Ballard. The first of these sources is R. D. Laing's book, *The Politics of Experience*.[15] The other source is the metaphysical writings of Aldous Huxley, including various of his essays together with *The Doors of Perception*[16] and *Heaven and Hell*.[17]

In common with Jung (and with Eliade and Campbell as well), Laing distinguishes between "ego" and "self." The former he characterizes as our bio-survival identity, a mode of awareness restricted by time and space, conditioned by culture, and dependent upon both inner and outer circumstances for its maintenance—circumstances as precarious as body chemistry or particular life situations such as being in love, having or not having a job, and so forth. The ego, according to Laing, is a self-validating but only very partial and limited mode of consciousness. It offers us a sense of ontological security but that security is an illusion. In reality, ego-consciousness constitutes "a state of sleep, of death, of socially accepted madness, a womb state to which one has to die, from which one has to be born."[18]

Laing further observes that we repress and resist the Self, or our inner identity, while desperately cultivating the ego, our instrument for adapting to the external world. And yet, at the same time, "society without knowing it, is *starving* for the inner," since our experience of the outer world "divorced from any illumination from the inner is . . . a state of darkness," a condition of "alienation or estrangement from the *inner light*."[19] Again, like Jung, Eliade, and Campbell, Laing views the evolutionary direction of consciousness as that of a movement from ego to Self, from the illusion of "identity-anchored, space-and-time-bound experience," to the experience of transcendence.[20] One way of accomplishing this journey, especially in the context of our secular, materialist culture, is to go mad. Madness, Laing observes, "need not be all break-down. It may also be break-through."[21]

There are some striking parallels between the writing of Laing and that of J. G. Ballard. Both share the notion that we are profoundly ambivalent with regard to our individual identities and our collective social identity, that we are clinging determinedly, apprehensively, to an illusion while at the same time forces within our psyches are working to overturn that illusion. Both writers also share the belief that "breakdown" and "break-through" are inextricably intertwined, that what may appear to be madness or disaster may be, as Laing phrases it, "veritable manna from heaven."[22] Further affinities of thought between Laing and Ballard will become evident in the course of my study.

Finally, I want to mention the influence that Aldous Huxley's metaphysical writings have exerted upon the perspective which I have brought to bear upon Ballard's work. Following the work of Henri Bergson and C. D. Broad, Huxley views ego-consciousness as a cerebral reducing-valve "shutting out most of what we should otherwise perceive or remember at any moment and leaving only that very small and special selection which is likely to be practically useful."[23] Beyond ego-identity, according to Huxley, there are higher, larger degrees of awareness, including what he calls the "not-I," which possesses "a greater power and a completer knowledge" than the ego-mind, as well as other unknown modes of consciousness that ultimately are identical with Universal Mind.[24]

As does Laing, Huxley emphasizes the deep ambivalence that we feel with regard to our ego-identity: "We love ourselves to the point of idolatry; but we also intensely dislike ourselves—we find ourselves unutterably boring. Correlated with this distaste for the idolatrously worshipped self, there is in all of us a desire, sometimes latent, sometimes conscious and passionately expressed, to escape from the prison of our individuality, an urge to self-transcendence."[25] This view of human consciousness expressed by Aldous Huxley possesses significant points of correspondence with that which is implicit in the fiction of J. G. Ballard. Both writers would, I believe, concur that ego-identity constitutes a perceptual filter and a prison, and that there are forces operative in the psyche that aim to abolish the filter and explode the prison.

Though I feel bound to acknowledge the inspiration that I have obtained from the above-named authors, it is from the fiction of J. G. Ballard that the true motive power of this study derives. My deepest motivation in writing this study is that Ballard's work excites and intrigues me. I find his fiction original and vital, and I consider him to be a major contemporary writer. I hope in the course of the following examination of Ballard's fiction to substantiate my claim for the importance of his work, and, at the same time, to impart to the reader something of the spirit of my own admiration for it.

A consideration of the ways in which Ballard's life may be related to his writing is entirely beyond the scope of this study, but some selected biographical data may perhaps be of interest to those readers who are unfamiliar with the author's background and the general outline of his career, and may also serve to suggest connections between Ballard's life in the world and the life of his imagination.

James Graham Ballard was born on November 15, 1930, in Shanghai, China, where his father was managing director for the Shanghai subsidiary of a Manchester firm of textile manufacters. The family lived in the International Settlement of the city, and young Ballard attended the Cathedral School. Already as a child, Ballard began to write adventure stories for his own amusement and as a ruse to fill out his copybook when he was assigned pages to copy as a punishment for infractions of classroom discipline. At the age of eleven, fascinated by the mysterious codes of Contract Bridge, Ballard produced a short study of the game in an edition of one hand-written copy. During this same period, from 1937 to the early 1940s, he also witnessed various incidents and effects of the Sino-Japanese war: artillery and aerial bombardments, battlefields outside the city strewn with the bodies of dead soldiers and pack animals.

In 1942, shortly after the outbreak of war between the Empire of Japan and the Allies, the Ballard family was interned by the Japanese in a civilian prisoner-of-war camp at Lunghua, where they remained until the end of the war. The following year, 1946, Ballard was, at the age of fifteen, "repatriated" to England, a country he had never before seen. In comparison with the exoticism and vitality of Shanghai and the intensity and the uncommon character of his experiences in the camp, it seemed to him to be very dull, and he felt himself to be something of an outsider.

Ballard attended the Leys School in Cambridge, disliking it intensely, and later enrolled in Cambridge University, reading medicine at King's College with the intention of becoming a psychiatrist. After completing the pre-clinical phase of his studies, however, Ballard lost interest and abruptly changed course, leaving Cambridge for London University, and switching from medicine to English. After a year at London University he abandoned his studies altogether, taking a series of odd jobs, including working as a Covent Garden porter and as an encyclopedia salesman, and writing copy for an advertising agency.

It was during this restless, intellectually fertile period, at King's College and afterward, that Ballard began to sense his vocation as a writer, trying his hand at various forms of short fiction, from the experimental to literary pastiche, and publishing his first story, "The Violent Noon," in the Cambridge *Varsity*. During these years he also pursued ardent interests in psycho-analysis and in surrealism. A self-timer-released, double-exposure photographic self-portrait taken by Ballard in Cambridge in 1950 shows two images of himself contemplating each other across a divan in a small room.[26] The self-portrait may be seen as inadvertently suggestive of Ballard's unsettled, irresolute state of mind at the time. It may also be seen to prefigure the self-divided protagonists so characteristic of his fiction, and perhaps also his fascination with overcoming the limitations of time.

A turning point for Ballard as a writer occurred during the period of his military service with the Royal Air Force in Canada, when he encountered American science fiction magazines for the first time, recognizing that in the science fiction medium he had at last found an appropriate vehicle for his imagination. Just before the end of his term of service, Ballard wrote "Passport to Eternity," his first science fiction story. Though it remained unpublished for several years, it seemed to confirm his new direction as a writer. Shortly after his discharge from the RAF, Ballard married Helen Mary Matthews, and thereafter began work as an editor for various technical and trade journals, eventually becoming assistant editor of the periodical, *Chemistry and Industry*.

Ballard began to publish science fiction stories with the British periodical, *New Worlds*, in 1956, writing his stories during stolen moments at work or evenings at home. In 1960, during his two-week annual holiday, Ballard wrote the novel, *The Wind from Nowhere*, with the hope of establishing himself as a professional writer. The maneuver proved to be successful and with the publication of *The Wind from Nowhere* in 1962, together with the appearance of collections of his short stories, Ballard was finally in a position to pursue writing on a full-time basis, though family responsibilities—the Ballards had three children—continued to occupy much of his time and energy, especially after the untimely death of his wife in 1964.

During the course of the 1960s, Ballard attained the position of a leading innovator in the science fiction medium, becoming a central figure in the British "New Wave" movement of s-f writers—of which I shall have more to say at a later point. By the end of the decade, the initial liberating appeal of science fiction for Ballard had begun to pall somewhat and his writing came to assume more and more its own very individual character, independent of all categories and conventions.

During the seventies and the eighties, Ballard's art has continued to evolve and to refine itself according to its own inner principles and imperatives, heedless of the canons of literary fashion or popular taste. Books such as *The Atrocity Exhibition* and *Crash* have been met with disapprobation or with blank incomprehension on the part of many readers and reviewers, while they have provoked outright hostility on the part of editors and publishers. At the same time, Ballard's work has won the commendation of several leading contemporary writers, including the late Graham Greene, Susan Sontag, William S. Burroughs, and Anthony Burgess among others, while his integrity as a writer and the original quality of his vision have also proved increasingly attractive to a broad and international readership.

Ballard's greatest popular success to date has been his novel, *Empire of the Sun*, based upon his experiences in the Lunghua Internment Camp. It was shortlisted for the Booker Prize and was awarded the Guardian Fiction Prize in 1984. The novel also served as the basis for a film directed by Steven Spielberg.

Despite growing appreciation for his work, Ballard continues to be a disturbing, unassimilated presence in contemporary English letters. The author's most recent fiction continues to be shaped by forces that *turn from beneath*, forces that assail all forms of stasis and complacency and that urge transformation and transcendence. With no diminishment of the wit, panache, and quirky grace that have distinguished his writing, and with a more mature control and a surer sense of his art, Ballard's latest works attest to the unrelentingly subversive character of his imagination.

1

The Dimension of the Disaster: The Early Short Fiction

J. G. Ballard's first published story, "The Violent Noon,"[1] appeared in the *Varsity* (Cambridge) in 1951, sharing the magazine's first prize of ten pounds for its Crime Story Competition. Although it is not, strictly speaking, a piece of juvenilia—the author was twenty-one years old at the time of writing—"The Violent Noon" is obviously an early effort, an apprentice piece, lacking the facility and skill of Ballard's more mature work. Nevertheless, the story does display ability and it is of interest for its suggestion of the young author's concerns and for its prefiguration of motifs that are central to Ballard's later fiction.

Since "The Violent Noon" has never been reprinted and is not readily obtainable, I will summarize the plot of the story.

Riding in their chauffeured automobile on a jungle road in Malaysia, in about 1950, rubber planter Michael Allison, his wife and baby daughter, together with their friend, Hargreaves, are ambushed by guerrillas. Allison, the baby, and the Malayan chauffeur are killed outright by the guerrillas' fire; Mrs. Allison is disfigured in the ensuing wreck of the vehicle. Hargreaves manages to return fire, wounding one of the guerrillas and driving off the remainder. Rescued by a passing lorry, Hargreaves and Mrs. Allison are brought to safety. The subsequent criminal investigation of the incident is conducted by an English police inspector, named Brodie, who from the very outset seems absolutely confident of apprehending the guerrillas, despite the great difficulties presented by the case. True to his word, Brodie arrests his first suspect the next day. Asked to identify the suspect, Hargreaves expresses strong doubt, while Mrs. Allison unhesitatingly identifies the man as one of the assailants. The inspector shows himself to be utterly brutal in his methods of interrogation, savagely beating the suspect. The following day Brodie produces more suspects for identification. Although Mrs. Allison promptly and positively identifies them as the terrorists, Hargreaves fails to recognize any of them and believes them all to be innocent. Nevertheless, upon reflection, Hargreaves also positively identifies the men, reasoning that "These innocent men must pay for the deaths of others, yield their lives to give a little consolation to this grieving widow," and further rationalizing that their martyrdom will also serve to prevent the condemnation of "yet more pitiful souls to an ironic death, to the brutal fury of Brodie" (9).

Ballard's short, stark story is less a comment upon the moral ambiguities of colonialism and de-colonization than a depiction of universal brutality and ignorance. All of the parties of the tale, the guerrillas, the planters, the police, the Malays, and the Chinese alike, are caught in a vicious circle compounded of misunderstanding, mistrust, vengeance, and reciprocal atrocity. The larger context of the tale is the jungle in which the events unfold, a sort of Conradian "heart of darkness" which provides an ambient metaphor for the blind violence of the story.

"The Violent Noon" is significant for its introduction of the theme of illusion, an important element of Ballard's later fiction. The illusions we unquestioningly embrace (as do the guerrillas, Brodie, and Mrs. Allison) or to which we acquiesce (as does Hargreaves) constitute what may be seen as a prison within a prison. The larger prison is the natural world itself (here imaged by the jungle) with its implacable laws and its ceaseless, senseless struggle between life and death; while the inner, closer prison is the dungeon of illusion: the self-deceptions that we cultivate and the collective fictions that we inherit.

The story is also notable for its early treatment of the motif of catastrophe and its interest in the effect of disaster upon the psyche.

Indeed, the most vividly written sequence of "The Violent Noon" is the ambush scene and its immediate aftermath, which is described with an almost clinical detachment and yet with undertones of a macabre humor—as in the detail of Mrs. Allison's lisp caused by the loss of her front teeth during the wreck of the automobile.

Although "The Violent Noon" anticipates features of Ballard's later fiction it is uncharacteristically pessimistic. Implicit in the action and the atmosphere of the story is the sense of an absurd universe, of meaningless life in a merciless world. In this manner the story may be seen to represent a sort of prime meridian of negativity in the author's work, a void or zero of the spirit to which his subsequent writing is a response and of which, ultimately, it is a refutation.

Ballard's next published story marks the real beginning of his career as a writer. It is titled "Escapement"[2] and appeared in *New Worlds* in 1956. I am intrigued by the title "Escapement," which with its multiple meanings might well serve as a collective title for all of Ballard's fiction, uniting as it does in a single word the concepts of time and of escape, both of which are so central to Ballard's work.

The story itself is the first of many written by Ballard which are centered upon the idea of time as a trap in which consciousness is confined. So all-encompassing and so all-pervading a prison is time that under normal circumstances we are scarcely aware of the strict constraint in which we are held. "Escapement" proposes to recall our attention to the true nature of the time-trap through the presentation of a fanciful situation in which an anomalous time-loop, consisting of a fifteen-minute interval of linear time, repeats itself again and again in the manner of a broken record. No resolution to the problem—or to the larger predicament it encapsulates—is offered by the story other than a sort of cheerful resignation in respect of forces beyond our power to affect or to alter.

The theme of time as a prison is extended and developed in several subsequent stories of this period. In "Build-Up,"[3] later re-titled "Concentration City," an endless city is employed as a metaphor for time. The city is infinite, limitless in all directions, and it is curved in time and space, so that after travelling for twenty days in a single direction on the city transport system, the protagonist of the story arrives where he started, *when* he started. His quest for "free space" is utterly thwarted; there is no escape.

The image of prison is equated with time-consciousness in a literal as well as a figurative sense in "Chronopolis,"[4] which takes place in a post-technological future in which the measurement of time is taboo and unlawful. The prohibition of all calibrated timepieces is the result of a revolt in years past against "Central Time Control," the key controlling factor in an infinitely complex, rigorously regimented, dehumanized urban megapolis.

Conrad, the focus of the story, is obsessed with time and time measurement, building sun-dials, sandglasses, water clocks and eventually obtaining an illicit wristwatch. His final act of defiance is to repair the Master Clock of the Central Time Control. Sentenced to a term of twenty years in prison, Conrad is at first delighted to learn that the penitentiary is equipped with a clock. After only a few weeks, however, he is dismayed to discover "The clock's insanely irritating tick" (217). Conrad's life and fate recapitulate in miniature the human historical process with regard to time: the discovery and gradual improvement of time measurement, increasing precision, perfection, and then the growing awareness of the tyranny of time, its insidious, inevitable control and oppression, and the revelation of time's limiting, constricting, inflexible authority over consciousness.

The stories "Mr. F is Mr. F"[5] and "Time of Passage"[6] both explore the possibility of reversed time in relation to the human condition. In the first story a man regresses physically and mentally from mature manhood through adolescence, to childhood, babyhood, and then re-enters the womb. There, he continues to devolve, ultimately becoming an embryo at the time of implantation, and finally disappearing altogether: "the moment of his conception coinciding with the moment of his extinction, the end of his last birth with the beginning of his first death" (121).

"Time of Passage" further develops the idea of reversed time, tracing the course of an inverted death-to-birth life through its various mental and social stages. In both stories the device of inversion serves to point up the implacable character of time, its supreme determining influence upon our being. Whether it moves backwards or forwards, time remains a prison.

That a method of escape from the prison of time may be possible is hinted at obliquely in "Time of Passage." Reversing a notion from William Wordsworth's famous "Ode: Intimations of Immortality from Recollections of Early Childhood," Ballard depicts the consciousness of the new-born dead as being suffused with a sense of eternity that lends a profoundity to their thoughts and actions until this visionary awareness gradually becomes dissipated, then lost altogether in the distractions of the world. Nevertheless, the story implicitly suggests the possibility of a non-time-dominated consciousness, though how such a mode of being might be maintained or achieved is not indicated.

Scientific advances and technical ingenuity are of no avail as tools of escape from time, according to Ballard's fiction, nor can they help to mitigate the loss and death attendant upon our captivity in time. In "The Gentle Assassin"[7] a man returns to the past in an attempt to alter a fateful historical event, only to become the inadvertent agency of its fulfillment. Time is thus shown to be relentless, unyielding; human fate in time inevitable, unavoidable. The prison is perfect.

Two other Ballard stories from this period which sustain the image of humankind's imprisonment in time are "Prisoner of the Coral Deep"[8] and "The Lost Leonardo."[9] The first story deals again with a time-traveller, in this instance "a mariner from the distant future, marooned millions of years ago," and unable to return to his own age. His "faint human cry, a stricken plea for rescue" (27), is preserved in a fossil shell found upon a beach in our present age by a passerby who narrates the story. This haunting image of helplessness, lostness and desperation serves as a symbol of our common human predicament, for in a sense we are all time-travellers, lost in time, unable to return home. The time-mariner's stricken cry, his desperate plea for rescue is an echo of our own silent cry for deliverance from time.

Another prisoner of time appears in "The Lost Leonardo," the mythic figure Ahasuerus, also known as the Wandering Jew. Ahasuerus, it will be remembered, was condemned to wander the face of the earth until the Second Coming in punishment for having taunted Christ bearing the cross toward Golgotha. Ballard employs Ahasuerus as an emblem of all humankind, condemned to endure time for having denied eternity in favor of the temporal, material world. In Ballard's story Ahasuerus is repeatedly compared to an angel albeit a "half-crippled angel" (220). He is a "fugitive through time and space" (210) seeking to redeem the eternal or "angelic" aspect of his being from the finite.

In contrast to the hopelessness of the situation of the prisoner in the foregoing story, Ahasuerus possesses the potential for deliverance from time and he works diligently toward that end. Through his skillful, meticulous altering of all the extant portraits of his face and figure, Ahasuerus is striving symbolically to effect an inner transformation that will release him from his malediction. In the latest of his altered self-portraits, painted upon a priceless da Vinci canvas of the crucifixion, Ahasuerus revises his depiction—originally that of an arrogant man, impatient with the suffering of the crucified figure, face half-averted from the scene in disgust—to one of a humble and compassionate man looking "upwards to the cross, a hint of hope, even of redemption in his wistful gaze" (221). Clearly, the author has begun to consider the possibility of redemption from time through altered consciousness as a feasible possibility, not only for Ahasuerus but by extension for all of us other accursed, half-crippled, human angels.

Time is not the only prison treated of in Ballard's writing. A deeper, closer prison is that of the mind, or, more precisely, that of the ego with its confining walls of fear and guilt, selfishness and narcissism, ambition and the lust for power. Bound up by its very nature with the temporal, material world, ego-consciousness constitutes a primary impediment to the transcendence of time. The sterile, truncated character of such consciousness provides the subject for a series of Ballard's early stories.

The stories "Now Zero,"[10] "The Man on the 99th Floor,"[11] and "A Question of Re-entry"[12] delineate extremes of egotism: civilized men who in their ruthless pursuit of self-aggrandizement succumb to the most primitive and vicious impulses, who aspire to absolute power, and who are driven to kill those standing in the way of their overweening ambitions. In each instance their malicious actions ultimately react upon themselves and they are either defeated or destroyed.

Time-consciousness and ego-consciousness are shown to be mutually reflective in "A Question of Re-entry," in which a renegade American journalist named Ryker sets himself up as a sort of deity among a tribe of Indians in the Amazon basin by means of an alarm clock and a copy of a table of satellite traverses. Ryker, who conceives of himself as a romantic figure in the tradition of Paul Gauguin, a refugee from civilization, is revealed to be a covert megalomaniac and a callous and obtuse impostor. He utterly fails to recognize or to comprehend the truer, deeper sense of time—a time marked by the ebb and flow of life—possessed by the tribe which he dominates, exploits and helps to destroy:

> the Indians were at equilibrium with their environment, accepting its constraints and never seeking to dominate the towering arbors of the forest, in a sense an externalization of their own psyches. Ryker had upset that equilibrium, and by using the Echo satellite had brought the 20th century and its psychopathic projections into the heart of the Amazonian deep, transforming the Indians into a community of superstitious and materialistic sightseers. (38)

The figure of Ryker recalls that of Kurtz, the corrupted idealist of Joseph Conrad's *Heart of Darkness*, and in a sense Ryker may also be seen as a shabby, contemporary parallel to the serpent in the Garden of Eden. Motivated by his blind egotism, Ryker re-enacts the temptation of humankind, precipitating the fall of what is perhaps the last original, innocent race of men and women into the world of time.

Ballard upholds the classic hubris-nemesis mechanism with regard to egotism, viewing retribution not only as an equal and

opposite reaction to selfishness, but suggesting, too, that an unconscious desire for the destruction of the isolate ego may be latent in
the nature of the psyche. Certainly a note of warning is recurrent
in the stories, and later in the novels, that we ignore the unconscious at our peril. Ballard's fiction suggests repeatedly that the
unconscious mind does not share the same values and goals as the
ego, and that although it may be subdued or excluded for a term,
in the long run it is more potent than the ego.

A further instance of the futility of the desires and appetites of
the ego occurs in "The Sound Sweep."[13] In this parable-like story
selfishness and ambition are embodied by Madame Giocanda, an
aging classical opera singer, formerly celebrated and renowned but
now hopelessly outmoded and forgotten in a world of ultrasonic
musical entertainment. Her counterpart is a mute named Mangon,
a selfless and devoted admirer of her art.

There is, in the course of the story, a short-lived reciprocity and
mutuality between the singer and the mute, but the potential
complementarity of their relationship is terminated through the
exorbitant vanity and vicious self-interest of the diva who betrays
and rejects her humble, loyal helpmate. For such arrogance and
cruelty the punishment exacted of Madame Giocanda is nothing
less than the fulfillment of her deepest and worst fears: the effective
loss of her singing voice together with her definitive rejection by
the music world. Her longed-for performance, her chance for a
come-back, ends as a "grotesque . . . insane parody of a classical
soprano" (77), and she is hooted and derided by the audience.

The story may be read as another indictment of egotism, an
illustration of the process by which the ego in striving to achieve
its highest, fullest gratification insures, instead, the realization of
its most appalling fears.

In a similar manner, "The Singing Statues"[14] deals with the
psychopathology of self-love and its limiting, destructive consequences. Lunora Goalen, the subject of the story, is a former movie
star, wealthy and famous, a sort of younger and more glamorous
version of Madame Giocanda. Although she is a strikingly beautiful woman, there is "a dead glaze in her slateblue eyes" (77) and

a curious aura about her of "something unhealthy," the suggestion of "a secret vice" (78).

Lunora's hidden malady proves to be narcissism; she is in love with herself, enamoured of her own beauty and dependent upon all that flatters her self-image. Purchasing a sonic sculpture under the mistaken impression that it is responding to her personally, she becomes addicted to its musical adulation, which is, in fact, entirely false, nothing more than a series of tape recordings which the sculptor has surreptitiously inserted into the statue. When Lunora discovers the deception she destroys the sculpture.

Lunora is from the outset incapable of responding to the statue on its own terms but is sensible of it only to the degree that it serves as a mirror reflecting the illusory self she seeks so desperately to sustain. Her morbid obsession with her own beauty and her sterile self-love preclude the possibility of her perceiving greater, truer beauty (that of art, the sculpture) or of experiencing real love (the rejected love of the sculptor). Hers is a prison of mirrors, sealing her off from life, both the life of the world and life within. The "dead glaze" of her eyes, together with the mortuary imagery of her secretary and her chauffeur, confirms the living death of such a constricted existence. Appropriately, the sculpture which she dismembers is topped with a set of wings, the emblem of transcendence, an aspiration that is inconceivable to her illusion-bound consciousness.

The conflict between the complex of desires and fears that cause us to cling to ego-mind and the irrepressible, unconscious compulsion to burst apart the confining boundaries of the ego constitutes the theme of "Thirteen to Centaurus."[15] The story is a sort of inverted parallel to Plato's allegory of the cave. The cave in this instance is a counterfeit spaceship which is thought by the members of its crew to be fifty years into an interstellar journey, but which is, in reality, resting in a hanger on earth, the object of a psychological experiment.

Despite the compulsory mental conditioning, employing post-hypnotic suggestion, that is intended to discourage curiosity and to distort perception among the members of the crew of the ship, an aged pilot and a young boy eventually discover the truth of their situation. Significantly, they choose not to inform the other crew members nor to attempt to escape from the illusion. They remain "inside" for reasons of personal ambition, preferring to manipulate a fraudulent but manageable "reality" rather than daring the larger reality of the world outside the ship. As one of the psychologists involved in the study of the closed community of the ship observes: "the people in the dome do *not* want to come out. Given the choice they would prefer to stay there, just as the gold-fish prefers to stay in its bowl" (26).

The only resistance to the enclosed world of the ship arises from the unconscious. The boy, Abel, is subject to a recurrent nightmare which even Dr. Francis, the ship psychologist, is helpless to cure. Abel's dream is of "a small disc of burning light that . . . expanded until it filled his brain like a thousand arc lights. It seemed endlessly distant, yet somehow mysteriously potent and magnetic, arousing dormant areas of his mind close to those which responded to his mother's presence" (13). This powerful, ambiguous image (which prefigures that of the sun in *The Drowned World*) suggests the life-giving, ego-destroying experience of the numinous. Coincidentally, perhaps, the predicament of Abel, caught between the constricted, unnatural but familiar world of the ship and the insistent urging of his nightmare, recalls Hamlet's remark: "I could be bounded in a nut-shell and count myself a king of infinite space; were it not that I have bad dreams" (*Hamlet*, Act 2, Scene 2).

A concomitant theme to the ego as prison is that of the prison of illusion. Two stories of this period concerned with the construction of prisons of the mind are "The Watch Towers"[16] and "End Game."[17] In the first story the illusion out of which the inner dungeon is built is guilt; in the second story it is innocence. In both stories the hapless protagonists are made prisoners of a self-invented "reality" that traps them, enclosing them in increasingly narrow cells of obsession. In the end, liberty, individuality, life itself are forfeit to illusion.

The problem of illusion also informs the story "Minus One,"[18] in which Ballard portrays the motives that cause and sustain illusion and the intense resistance of illusion to correction or contradiction.

Appropriately, the story is set at Green Hill Asylum, a maximum-security mental institution of the sort that, as the narrator informs us, "in effect serve the role of private prisons" (95). After the escape of a patient named James Hinton, and following a futile search for him, the director of the asylum, Dr. Mellinger, manages by means of sophistry and deceitful cunning to persuade the other members of his staff that James Hinton never existed, arguing that "a vast edifice of fantasy was erected around the wholly mythical identity of one patient" (101).

In so doing Mellinger is motivated by the fear of losing his position with all its power and status, while in accepting his explanation as valid the members of the asylum staff are likewise motivated by the fear of blame, disgrace, and ruined careers. The irony of the situation lies in their real belief in Mellinger's explanation, and in Mellinger's apparent ability to accept his own preposterous invention. Indeed, so staunch is their belief in the lie that when Mrs. Hinton suddenly and unexpectedly appears at the asylum, having come to visit her husband, they are able to dismiss her as "suffering from terrible delusions," since "Hinton never existed" (102). In this manner they dispose of the threat she poses to their cherished and necessary illusion. The ending of the story suggests that Mrs. Hinton will be involuntarily committed to the asylum for "treatment" by the doctors.

In like manner, whatever is inconvenient, unacceptable or otherwise inimical to the ego is subdued and excluded from consciousness, its expression stifled except through dreams or through other irruptions of the unconscious. Ultimately, however, the point is reached when the illusions of the ego can no longer be maintained before the intense pressure of the unconscious and they must then give way or be shattered. The occurrence of this latter event constitutes the subject of a number of Ballard's subsequent fictions.

Since much of Ballard's fiction is diagnostic, setting forth the terms of the human predicament—trapped in time and the material world—or hortative, warning us of the pitfalls of ego and illusion, it has frequently been assumed that the author's vision is pessimistic, fatalistic, even nihilistic. Such a view overlooks the central concern of Ballard's writing with the problem of transcendence, with exceeding the limitations of material, temporal being and ordinary ego-consciousness. Ballard may truly be said to be pessimistic only with regard to the transitory nature of physical existence, the material universe and finite time. It is precisely these conditions that lend such urgency and such importance to the quest for transcendence in his work.

Already in "Build-up" ("The Concentration City"), one of Ballard's earliest stories, the urge for transcendence is manifested in the protagonist's dream of flight in free space, in a place where: "There were no walls. Nothing but emptiness" (33). This dream inspires him to build a flying machine and to embark upon a quest for free space, a quest, however, thwarted by the infinite nature of the city which proves to be co-extensive in scope and duration with space and with time.

Fuller and somewhat more optimistic treatments of the theme of transcendence are to be found in the stories "The Waiting Grounds"[19] and "The Voices of Time."[20] The first story represents Ballard's broadest vision of time, describing the process of the great cosmic cycle, the evolution of the universe: beginning as primal gas and dust, the cosmos proceeds through a material, temporal stage to become ultimately a disembodied wave of ideation which approaches pure sentience only to collapse upon itself, disintegrating into a debris of energy out of which the next cosmic cycle begins. In this manner, we are told, the universe "has ended and regenerated itself an infinite number of times" (74) but has ever failed to attain to pure being, to transcend itself.

The title of the story refers to a remote planet in another galaxy on which four stellar races have gathered. Here they have created a series of inscribed megaliths, and are waiting in anticipation of the advent of "a cosmic redeemer" (74). The handful of human settlers who also occupy the planet, engaged in scientific and commercial endeavors, are entirely oblivious to the higher purposes the planet serves until the discovery of the megaliths by two of their number, Mayer and Tallis. Mayer embodies the kind of ego-consciousness with which we are familiar from other Ballard stories. He is ruthlessly ambitious, materialistic, utterly indifferent to the spiritual significance of the megaliths, concerned only with their potential for commercial exploitation as precious metal. When Tallis objects to his plans and attempts to dissuade him from them, Mayer tries to kill him.

Tallis, on the other hand, embodies the nobler aspirations of humankind. After having proved his good faith to the unseen watchers, the builders of the megaliths, he is initiated into the meaning of the megaliths through a vision of the great cosmic cycle. His name is inscribed on one of the megaliths and he joins the vigil in wait for the cosmic redeemer. The struggle enacted between Mayer and Tallis represents at a micro-cosmic level a parallel to the ongoing struggle of the cosmos to evolve from finite matter and finite consciousness to pure, infinite being. The story concludes on a note of optimism with Tallis's sense of confidence that the revelation is imminent, and that whatever its precise nature, "it must be worth waiting for" (74).

In one sense the story "The Voices of Time" seems to reverse the essential motifs of "The Waiting Grounds," replacing the former story's sense of joyous expectation of a cosmic event with a sense of dread anticipation, and replacing the hopeful approach of a new beginning with the relentless approach of an inevitable end. In a deeper sense, though, the stories are not as unlike as they may at first seem, and may even be considered as the same story seen from two different perspectives.

Catastrophes in "The Voices of Time" overlap and mirror each other: the narcoma syndrome, biological entropy, and the impending termination of the universe. From the cellular level to the cosmic the countdown is running, and the end is approaching.

The narrative focus of the story is upon Dr. Powers, a scientist terminally ill with the narcoma syndrome, his periods of consciousness steadily diminishing. Power's reaction to his ever-dwindling amount of time and consciousness is to seek to escape time, to exceed its dominion. Both his decision and the actions he undertakes to implement it seem to be dictated by his unconscious mind. Powers commences his endeavor by throwing away his alarm clock and his wristwatch. Compulsively and only half-aware of what he is doing, he embarks upon the construction of a mandala in the desert. Powers begins to live according to an inner, deeper, psychic time. Subsequently, he undergoes a further change of temporal orientation, conceiving of the world around him according to a vaster scale of time, becoming preternaturally aware of the landscape in terms of geologic time:

> Not only could he see the escarpment, but he was aware of its enormous age, felt distinctly the countless millions of years since it had first reared itself out of the magma of the earth's crust. . . . It seemed to Powers that he could feel the separate identity of each sand-grain and salt-crystal calling to him from the surrounding ring of hills. (38–29)

Powers then begins to sense and to participate in the even more immense scale of cosmic time, the millennia of stars, nebulae and galaxies. Finally, situating himself at the center of his mandala, he relinquishes consciousness of time altogether to become united with the very source of time and the source of the cosmos itself:

> he felt its massive magnetic pull, let himself be drawn into it, borne gently on its powerful back. Quietly, it carried him away, and he rotated slowly, facing the direction of the tide. Around him the outlines of the hills and the lake had faded, but the image of the mandala, like a cosmic clock, remained fixed before his eyes, illuminating the broad surface of the stream. Watching it constantly, he felt his body gradually dissolving, its physical dimensions melting into the vast continuum of the current, which bore him out into the centre of the great channel, sweeping him onward beyond hope but at last at rest, down the broadening reaches of the river of eternity. (39–40)

Powers's counterpart and alter-ego in the story is Kaldren, who remains bound to ego-consciousness—he can't even relinquish it to sleep, having undergone narcotomy—and bound to linear, quantitative time. It is significant to the larger dimension of meaning suggested by his character that the sign with which he is associated in the story is $\sqrt{-1}$, an impossible number, a dead-end exercise in utter futility. Powers's sign, in contrast, is the mandala that he constructs, and by which he unites both circle and line, effecting a symbolic marriage of linear and cyclic time, of the finite and the infinite.

The ending of the story seems to imply a sort of continuity, as Kaldren recalls the dead Powers and his mandala in much the same manner as, at the beginning of the story, Powers recalled his dead predecessor, Whitby, who had constructed a mandala during the last months of his life. This cyclic symmetry of structure may serve to suggest an eventual redemption from time and from ego-mind for Kaldren.

Another attempt by an individual to liberate himself from time and the material universe occurs in the story "The Overloaded Man."[21] The main character of the story, Faulkner, has developed a mental ability to de-identify and dissociate from sensory input, seeking by this means to escape from the external world into "an absolute continuum of existence uncontaminated by material excrescences" (92). Faulkner's efforts ultimately result in the unintentional slaying of his wife and in his own suicide. Despite his determination, the flawed character of the protagonist is incapable of true transcendence, and he attains only solipsism and extinction. The urge for transcendence is clearly present in Faulkner but the necessary spiritual qualities are entirely lacking.

In "The Garden of Time"[22] the author portrays a transcendence of another character entirely, a transcendence of time achieved through love and the contemplation of beauty. The protagonists of the story, Count Axel and his wife (an allusion to the play *Axel* by Villiers de l'Isle-Adam), are ultimately themselves transformed into objects of enduring beauty, thereby escaping the destructiveness of the temporal world, which is represented by an army of vicious and ignorant vandals encroaching upon their elegant villa.

One of Ballard's most numinous images of transcendence occurs in his story "The Time Tombs."[23] The powerful and mysterious image of the dead princess, depicted in terms of light and flight, serves to oppose the story's contending cluster of imagery of erosion and death: sand, decay, the time-tombs. In a corresponding manner, the characters of Shepley and Traxel oppose each other; the former anguished, confused but earnest in his quest for understanding and meaning; the latter mocking, cynical, unscrupulous, and utterly selfish.

The central issues of the story are those of life and immortality, whether of a specious or of a genuine nature. The time-tombs with their tapes of coded personalities recorded in hope of eventual resurrection are an expression of vanity. They represent the desire for a false "immortality" of the ego in the realm of time. In contrast, the tomb of the princess symbolizes a transcendental immortality, serving as a sign of a realm beyond time and death, "where archetypal beings of superhuman stature glimmered in their own self-generated light" (28). Significantly, since the ego and its narrow vision constitute an impediment to transcendence and true immortality, the tomb of the princess does not contain tapes of her personality. Her aim, we may infer on the basis of the spiritual character of the imagery in which she is depicted, was an infinitely higher form of resurrection than that of the ego-identity.

In the course of the story Shepley undergoes a metamorphosis, we may even say a spiritual resurrection. From being self-destructive, brooding, and morose (a potential Traxel), he becomes reverently aware of and dedicated to higher purposes in life. His calm acceptance of his punishment—indeed, his insistence upon it— when he is caught by the time-wardens at the end of the story bespeaks a new commitment to values beyond those of ego. When questioned by the time-wardens concerning the looted tapes, he dismisses the tapes as being "just the persona . . . The empty skin" (34). This statement indicates a belief in a transcendent essence that surpasses the limits of mind and of physical existence. Although Shepley does not himself attain transcendence, he is clearly on the right path to that end. For him imprisonment may represent a mode of penance and of liberation.

The penitential ordeal of the Ballard hero in quest of transcendence receives more extended treatment in "The Terminal Beach"[24] and "The Delta at Sunset."[25] The first story concerns the pilgrimage of a man named Traven to the island of Eniwetok, where he lives like an ascetic among the abandoned concrete bunkers and towers and the relics and ruins of atomic weapons tests. Traven has been impelled by forces in his unconscious to journey to the island in quest of his dead wife and child, who were killed in an automobile accident, and, in the furtherance of that end, to achieve liberation from time and ego-identity.

Traven systematically divests himself of all superfluities, all inessentials, reducing himself to the bedrock of consciousness. He endures extremes of privation and suffering, sustained in his self-imposed ordeal by glimpses of his wife and son, fleeting visions which gradually become clearer and approach nearer. By degrees, too, he frees himself of time, proceeding from quantative to quantal time. By the climax of the story he has recognized in the desolate landscape of the island "an ontological Garden of Eden," where he can at last attain to an identity "free of the hazards of time and space" (153). The story concludes with Traven patiently awaiting imminent reunion with his family, whose specters are now only a few yards distant.

The process of breaking through the boundaries that separate the conscious mind from the timeless realm of the unconscious is also central to "The Delta at Sunset." Although the overt situation of the story is almost a pastiche of Ernest Hemingway's "The Snows of Kilimanjaro," Ballard's story is closer in spirit to Arthur Rimbaud's famous dictum about becoming a seer by means of a systematic derangement of the senses. In this instance, the derangement of the senses of the protagonist, Charles Gifford, is occasioned by a fever stemming from an infected foot. Yet the fever and the infection are less the cause of Gifford's visions (or hallucinations, as his wife calls them) than are his own deep-rooted, unconscious need and desire for them.

Gifford refuses to acquiesce in the "obsessive time-consciousness" of Western civilization, and aspires, instead, to identify himself with the "flux of nature" (118). Having already succeeded in rejecting the body before the onset of his illness, Gifford is discouraged to discover that it is not the flesh "that ties us to mortality but our confounded egos" (118). It is out of this impasse that the visions are born, subverting his ego-mind and supplanting it with primordial consciousness.

Under the tutelary guidance of the totemic serpents and the mandalas of his visions, Gifford leaves behind quotidian reality "where events moved on a single plane of time like the blurred projection of a three-dimensional object by a defective camera obscura" (121). Proceeding by degrees, he enters "a zone of complete timelessness" (125) and "a world of absolute values" (129).

Common to the protagonists of both "The Terminal Beach" and "The Delta at Sunset"—and to a significant extent also to the protagonist of "The Voices of Time"—is a pattern or process that consists of a rejection of commonplace reality and of time; a rejection of the body, accompanied by a mortification of the flesh or the undergoing of an ordeal; the gradual establishing of contact with a primordial, mythic reality that is innate and latent in the psyche; and, finally, the acceptance of death as a transcendence of the false, shallow identity of the ego and of the equally spurious and superficial reality of the material, temporal world, and as an entrance into a realm of timeless absolutes.

The role of the unconscious in the process of transcendence, as it is depicted in Ballard's work, is obviously a vital one, with the unconscious representing both a source of energy and guidance and a communicating link with the realm of transcendent reality. The function of the unconscious in Ballard's fiction is most often subversive, undermining and overthrowing the fixities of the rational intelligence and the ego. The conceptualization of the unconscious that is implicit in Ballard's writing is one that would seem to possess significant affinities with that of Carl Jung, in that it is viewed as being composed of both a personal unconscious and a collective unconscious. The latter is, in turn, connected to the natural world and ultimately to universal mind. The nature of the relationship between the conscious, rational mind and the unconscious, their opposition, competition and mutual resistance, is a recurrent theme in several of the author's stories from this period and throughout his work.

"Manhole 69"[26] is an early representation of the conflict between the conscious and the unconscious aspects of the psyche, in which an experimental operation to eliminate the need for sleep goes amiss, resulting in catatonic seizures for the subjects of the experiment. The cause of their extreme psychological reaction is that continual consciousness drives the mind to unendurable limits of self-awareness; the subjects "could no longer contain the idea of their own identity" (168). They are, in effect, overwhelmed by their own intensified ego-consciousness. Significantly, the subjects come to imagine themselves as being tightly confined in time and space, experiencing in literal terms the close prison of the ego.

The scientist responsible for the operation, Dr. Neill, consistently denigrates and dismisses the unconscious, characterizing it as a "sump" and as "marshland" to be reclaimed by the conscious mind. He states that "The further we hold back the unconscious, the better" (146). The events of the story, however, suggest that the unconscious is primary and essential to our identity, that its power exceeds that of the conscious mind, and that all that serves to separate or to sunder us from the unconscious is pernicious. The unconscious is, in the chess metaphor of the story, enthroned in the psyche as "the black king" (165).

Another aspect of the conflict between the rational intelligence of the ego and the sur-rational intelligence of the unconscious is set forth in "The Thousand Dreams of Stellavista,"[27] in which the "bioplastic" and "psychotropic" house purchased by Howard and Fay Talbot may be seen as a metaphor for the psyche, with the original inhabitants of the house, Gloria Tremayne and Miles Vanden Starr, seen to represent aspects of the psyche, the unconscious and the rational ego-mind, respectively. During the period of their residence in the house the feminine principle embodied by Gloria was dominated, persecuted and menaced by the aggressive masculine principle embodied by Miles. In self-defense, she was finally driven to kill him.

Due to the "psychotropic" nature of the house, the new owners, Howard and Fay, are compelled by the encoded personalities of Gloria and Miles to re-enact the traumatic events of the past, made unwittingly and unwillingly to assume the roles of the former inhabitants. Howard succeeds, however, in confronting and overthrowing the masculine presence, and the story concludes with his intention to cultivate the feminine aspect of the house, by which he is deeply intrigued and enchanted. In this way, the story twice affirms the victory of the unconscious over the usurping ego.

Rather more equivocal victories of the unconscious are portrayed in "Now Wakes the Sea"[28] and in "The Reptile Enclosure."[29] In the former story a man who is convalescing from an illness (and whose ego-sustaining psychic energies are therefore temporarily in abeyance) is subject to recurrent night visions in which he sees the waters of an ancient sea encroaching upon the houses and streets of the suburban community in which he lives. On a promontory at some distance above the tides of this midnight sea stands the figure of a woman whom night after night the protagonist, Mason, attempts to reach. When finally the ancient waters reach his house and he at last reaches the woman on her promontory, he falls to his death *in time past*.

"The Reptile Enclosure" modifies and extends the motif of the foregoing story with, in this instance, an immense congregation of bathers at an overcrowded beach suddenly and compulsively entering the sea to drown themselves en masse like lemmings.

Common to both stories is the image of the sea as a metaphor for the unconscious, and the depiction of the irresistible attraction that it exerts upon the human mind. Also, in both stories, although the surrender to this magical attraction is fatal, death under such circumstances is portrayed by the author as a fulfillment, a reversion to fundamental, primordial consciousness, a liberating return to the deepest level of being: the undifferentiated consciousness of "the great time womb . . . the universal time-sea" ("Reptile," 111).

In "The Gioconda of the Twilight Noon"[30] Ballard recasts the Oedipus myth as a parable of the struggle between the ego and the unconscious, employing again the motif of an irresistible attraction that ultimately overthrows the conscious mind. Ballard's revised, updated version of the myth reverses the significance of the self-inflicted blindness of the hero from that of representing an act of self-punishment, of despair and defeat, to that of representing an act of liberation.

The protagonist of the story, Richard Maitland, recovering from a minor eye operation, discovers during his temporary blindness the inner eye of the unconscious. By means of this power he explores a rich and mysterious inner world in which "everything . . . is more real" (198). When at last the bandages are removed from his eyes and he regains his sight, Maitland experiences "A profound sense of loss" (200). The external world seems to him dull and "dead" (201) in comparison with the splendors and raptures of the inner world of the unconscious. Unwilling to endure exile from that visionary realm, he deliberately blinds himself, "an eager, unrepentant Oedipus" (201). Once more, the power of the unconscious proves more potent than the conscious mind.

Yet although Ballard repeatedly affirms the power of the unconscious, he by no means underestimates the tenacity and resourcefulness of the ego-mind and the rational intelligence. The mechanisms by which the conscious personality, in order to sustain its dominance, contrives to misapprehend, to misapply or to disregard the manifestations of the unconscious serve as the theme for two stories of this period: "The Venus Hunters"[31] and "The Drowned Giant."[32]

"The Venus Hunters" addresses the problem of construing the images communicated by the unconscious, warning that to comprehend their meaning at a literal level represents a fundamental error of interpretation that deflects us from their true significance. This is the nature of the mistake made in the story by an astronomer named Andrew Ward, who comes to be a sort of disciple to Charles Kandinski, a charismatic figure who claims to have seen and to have spoken with Venusians. Deeply skeptical at first, Ward eventually becomes a convert, even to the point of sharing one of Kandinski's visions of visitors from Neptune.

With his reductive scientific orientation, Ward fails utterly to perceive the symbolic dimension of what he and Kandinski experience, fails to understand that the alien landings are not real in the sense of being objective phenomena, but that their reality, their truth, is of another order entirely. In contrast to Ward, Professor Cameron, Ward's superior at the observatory, conceives of Kandinski as a true prophet, but in the sense that "the real significance of his fantasies . . . is to be found elsewhere than on the conscious plane, as an expression of the immense forces stirring below the surface of rational life . . ." (104).

By the very nature of each, the revelations of the unconscious are not to be assimilated by the rational mind. The images in which the energies of the unconscious are expressed are untranslatable; they must be understood according to their own terms or not at all.

The process of trivialization and denial of the marvelous and the numinous is detailed in a sequence of concise, resonant images in Ballard's key story, "The Drowned Giant." The drowned giant of the title embodies the kind of event that should occasion a profound and thorough-going re-examination of our world and of our identity, a re-evaluation of our paradigm of reality. Instead it serves to provide only a fleeting diversion from our daily round.

The initial reaction of the townspeople in the story upon hearing of the drowned giant is one of skepticism and disbelief. When confronted with the incontrovertible fact of his existence they feel a brief sense of awe and wonder which all too quickly passes over into a sort of contemptuous familiarity, followed by indifference. In the end the giant is largely forgotten, misremembered by the few who do recall the event as having been a huge sea beast that washed ashore, rather than a giant human being. From initial to final denial the potentially subversive information represented by the giant has been processed by the rational, conscious mind.

Throughout the story the giant is ennobled by the narrator (who alone comprehends the giant's significance) by comparisons with the heroic, the mythic, and the monumental. The giant is also characterized as a being out of "another world" (4), "a world of absolutes" (44), and "another dimension" (46). Allusions to the archaic, spiritual dimension of the giant are also made, including comparisons of parts of his body to "some water-lapped temple on the Nile" (41) and to the "megaliths of some primitive druidical religion" (49). Significantly, the aspect of the giant's size is reversed by the narrator so that the giant becomes the standard against which other human beings are measured. The narrator's fellow inhabitants of the city are thus seen as "diminutive" (40), "miniature" (44, 47), and as "puny copies" (44) of the original, primordial man embodied by the giant.

Considered in this perspective, the desecrations and abuses enacted upon the giant are the more contemptible, obtuse and impious. Each interest, each trade and professioin of the city—the curiosity seekers, the scientists, the representatives of the Department of Public Works, the circus proprietors, the commercial interests—can only conceive of the giant in terms of their own narrow values: as a diversion, an anomalous phenomenon, as so much fertilizer and cattle food, and so on.

The dismemberment and fragmentation of the giant may be seen to represent tactics of resistance employed by the rational, utilitarian ego against the status-quo-threatening revelations of the unconscious. (The giant appears out of the sea, a traditional symbol of the unconscious, and one employed previously by the author.) The title of the story may be ambiguous, referring not only to the particular drowned giant of the tale, but perhaps also to the giant within each of us whom we have drowned.

Two closely inter-related thematic concerns that recur in Ballard's fiction are technology and oppression, or more specifically, the various anti-human applications and consequences of technology, and the erosion of human intellectual and spiritual autonomy through forms of social systematization, manipulation, and control. Sometimes the two themes are treated together, at other times separately. Sometimes they provide the essential background of a particular story; at other times they constitute the main theme.

"Track 12"[33] is an early treatment of the use of technology to serve base ends, in this case personal revenge. A similarly egotistical desire, that of ambition, motivates the character of Fowler in "The Man on the 99th Floor,"[34] where a scientific technique is employed for purposes of murder. In "The Sound Sweep" and "Studio 5, the Stars"[35] technology encroaches upon the arts. In the first story the human singing voice has been superseded by ultra-sonic music; in the second the writing of poetry has been com-puterized, rendering all individual vision and voice obsolescent. In both instances the end result of this technological hegemony is a sterile, effete "art," utterly devoid of intensity, resonance, and human value.

A further, fuller treatment of the corrupting influence of tech-nology upon human needs and desires is to be found in "Passport to Eternity."[36] Set on an alien planet in the distant future, yet possessing unmistakable relevance to contemporary life, the story illustrates the way in which technological advances pander to the lowest aspects of the human character, while at the same time serving to stifle higher aspirations. The highly developed tech-nological gadgetry of the future consists in large part of what are merely games and toys for adults, complex forms of amusement and diversion, trivial and frivolous distractions from the essential existential issues of the human condition.

The citizens of the future society are depicted as bored and unfulfilled, stifled by status, by convention and by their own appetite for self-gratification. The travel and vacation agencies offer every conceivable form of ego-fulfillment, thereby inhibiting or perverting every impulse in the direction of personal growth, renewal and awareness. The ultimate price of this technological garden of earthly delights is living-death, as symbolized by the situation of the man and wife vacationers at the end of the story: confined as helpless, will-less prisoners, totally controlled, and with no hope of escape.

Future dystopias and semi-totalitarian states of one sort and another are a recurrent element in Ballard's fiction, most often conceived as direct extensions of the urbanization and industrial-ization processes or the ideologies of our own age. The author's earliest dystopian vision is that of "The Concentration City" (earlier title: "Build-up"), the ultimate megapolis: a multi-tiered world-city in which Pyros and Fire Police battle each other, a planet of concrete and asphalt inhabited by a race of quiescent conformists. A parallel vision is presented in "Billenium"[37] in which 95 percent of the world population lives in overcrowded cities, battling giant pedestrian jams in the streets, living in tiny cubicles of four square meters per person, and subject to systematic governmental reductions of allotted living space. In "Chronopolis" the author foresees that even if revolt against the dehumanizing regimentation of technological society should occur, it may well be succeeded by other forms of oppression, in this instance the Time Laws, the Time Police, and their agents.

"The Insane Ones"[38] envisions a society in which an ultra-conservative world government enacts Mental Freedom Laws which affirm "the individual's freedom to be insane" (117), and thereby criminalize all forms of psychotherapy or individual assistance or interference. The ultimate result of this legislation is the institutionalization of insanity, government by the truly mad, with a resultant police state that is characterized by intolerance and repressive control. An equally bleak vision is expressed in "The Subliminal Man,"[39] where Ballard depicts an urbanized, stand-ardized, manipulated consumerist society of the near future, a nightmare treadmill of mortgages, time payments, instant product obsolescence, status-seeking, inflation, and overwork. Subliminal manipulation, effectively assisted by violent police suppression, triumphs definitively over brief and limited resistance to the consumerist imperative. The final image of the story suggests the unchallenged ascendancy of a general state of death-in-life with "the shadows of the [subliminal] signs swinging over the heads of the people on their way to the supermarket like the blades of enormous scythes" (76).

Technology in the universe of Ballard's fiction may be seen as an extension of ego-mind, a set of implements with which to seize, to subdue or to slay for purposes of self-aggrandizement or self-gratification. Ballard's dystopias are likewise externalizations of ego-consciousness, of the appetites for pleasure and power, of fears and desires. The suppression of the arts or of other ego-threatening ideas, the subjugation of nature, and the oppression and manipulation of others, represent supreme and ultimate manifestations of the ego-mind's craving for security and dominance.

Accordingly, in the face of ever multiplying and ever more serious outrages inflicted by technology and by the agencies of oppression upon the human psyche and the natural world, madness and catastrophe become the only means by which the unconscious can resist and can assert itself against the despotism of ego-consciousness.

Although not yet a fully realized theme in Ballard's early short fiction, catastrophe already takes many forms: it may be personal or collective, manifesting itself as psychosis, disease, compulsion, ecological disaster or it may assume other guises. It may result from an illness or a wound as in "Now Wakes the Sea" and "The Delta at Sunset"; or it may be self-inflicted as in "The Terminal Beach" or "The Gioconda of the Twilight Noon." ⊬

The Pyros of "The Concentration City" represent a potential catastrophe; indeed with their obscure, apparently compulsive, motivation and their unmistakably destructive intent they represent the germ of a classic Ballardian catastrophe. Both the subjects of the narcotomy experiment in "Manhole 69" and the sunbathers in "The Reptile Enclosure" are victims of catastrophes that are directly attributable to latent forces of the unconscious. The mysterious narcoma syndrome of "The Voices of Time" may well share that same cause and origin.

That we are ultimately intercepted and overthrown by forces in our world or in ourselves which we have abused or rejected is suggested by two stories: "Zone of Terror"[40] and "Deep End."[41] In the first story a computer programmer named Larsen, an impatient, aggressive, unimaginative man engaged in programming "the complex circuitry of a huge brain simulator" (126) designed to simulate states of psychic dissociation, finds himself in precisely such a state. Larsen suffers a nervous breakdown during which he sees his double, his other self. Advised by his psychiatrist to confront the doppelganger, Larsen instead flees and hides in terror, and even attempts to kill his double with a revolver. In the end his double is the instrument of Larsen's own death.

In "Deep End" the thoughtless and greedy exploitation of the earth's natural resources has left the planet poisoned and moribund. The mining of the oceans has resulted in their death. The sole remnant of the earth's once vast and mighty oceans is Lake Atlantic "a narrow ribbon of stagnant brine ten miles in length by a mile wide" (161). Having despoiled their own planet and made it uninhabitable, human beings are now forced to flee to other planets.

The story emphasizes the profound relationship between the sea and the human psyche: "The seas are our corporate memory . . . we deliberately obliterated our own self-identities" (160). With the killing of the seas, the drying of the ocean floors, humankind has divorced itself from the very source of life, as well as symbolically from its own unconscious life. Thus "poet and dreamer . . . those species are extinct now" (160). In mortally wounding the planet we have inflicted identically corresponding wounds upon our own psyches.

The discovery of a last surviving fish in Lake Atlantic gives brief promise of renewal, hope for the advent of "new forms of life, a completely new biological kingdom" (165), even a "New Eden" (166). But the last fish, in common with the earth itself and all of its once myriad and multitudinous life forms, becomes the last victim of callous human destructiveness, of unthinking and uncaring egotism.

In essence, the terms of "Deep End" represent a précis of those which inform Ballard's other stoires of this period: the quest for a New Eden, or "an ontological Garden of Eden," as it is phrased in "The Terminal Beach" (153), in opposition to the narrow perception and heedless self-interest that characterize the ego-mind.

As I have attempted to demonstrate in this section, Ballard's early short fiction traces a series of key diagrams of the author's essential metaphysic. His overlapping, interlocking themes describe a crisis of consciousness that obtains at levels of the personal, the social and the universal. The consistent aim implicit in this body of work is to redeem the self from the ego, to deliver the human from repressive, reductive systems of control, and to liberate consciousness, both individual and collective, from confinement in the material, temporal universe.

A Catechism of Cataclysm: *The Wind from Nowhere, The Drowned World, The Drought, The Crystal World*

There is a Sufi aphorism to the effect that "When the mind weeps for loss, the spirit claps its hands with joy." This sense of radical duality inherent in the human make-up, of relentless and unyielding opposition between a superficial, external, conscious self and a deeper, unknown, true self, a self that is beyond the limits of our ordinary experience or understanding, possesses obvious affinities to Ballard's work, and provides a key to the understanding of the author's four novels of catastrophe. Ballard's visions of disaster, by flood, by drought, and so forth, are portrayed in such a manner that these events are seen to represent the deepest, most secret desires of humankind. It is not Thanatos, the instinctual desire for death, to which I allude here, but rather the desire for apocalypse, in the most literal sense of the word: a destruction that uncovers, a purifying process by which the false and evil are exposed and abolished and the "New Jerusalem" established.

Ballard has himself expressed such a view in his discussion of the cataclysms and dooms of science fiction literature: "Each one of these fantasies represents an arraignment of the finite, an attempt to dismantle the formal structure of time and space which the universe wraps around us at the moment we first achieve consciousness."[1] The disaster motif in Ballard's fiction is thus grounded, not in a nihilistic wish for extinction, but in the desire for transcendence.

Ballard's first novel of disaster, *The Wind from Nowhere*,[2] is altogether his most conventional and most uncharacteristic effort, adhering essentially to the canons of the catastrophe genre, though not entirely without certain quirky undertones. As the title suggests, the nature of the cataclysm is a global cyclone whose wind velocity ultimately reaches 550 mph, destroying nearly every surface structure on the face of the earth and inflicting untold millions of casualties.

A possible scientific explanation for the wind is offered at one point in the novel:

> Recently our monitors have detected unusually high levels of cosmic radiation. All electro-magnetic wave forms have mass—perhaps a vast tangential stream of cosmic radiation exploded from the sun during the solar eclipse a month ago, struck the earth on one exposed hemisphere, and its gravitational drag might have set in motion the huge cyclone revolving round the earth's axis at this moment. (48)

But, what is perhaps more to the point, it is also suggested that "it's the deliberate act of an outraged Providence, determined to sweep man and his pestilence from the surface of this once green earth" (48). Or, as it is further suggested, it is "Nature herself in revolt, in her purest, most elemental form" (141).

Certain features of the story combine to indicate that the cause of the wind may be something deeper and more mysterious than cosmic radiation. Among such indications perhaps the most suggestive are the circumstances of the duel between the character of Hardoon and the wind. Hardoon, the possessor of immense resources of wealth, power, technology, and energy, challenges the wind by having an enormous pyramid constructed during the hurricane, a gesture which to him represents the assertion of human reason and potency against the refractory fury of the natural world. As Hardoon himself expresses his personal defiance of the forces of nature:

> As the wind has risen so everyone on the globe has built downward, trying to escape it; has burrowed further and deeper into the shelter of the earth's mantle. With one exception—myself. . . . Only I, in the face of the greatest

holocaust ever to strike the earth, have had the moral courage to attempt
to outstare nature. That is my sole reason for building this tower. Here on
the surface of the globe I meet nature on her own terms, in the arena of
her choice. If I fail, Man has no right to assert his innate superiority over
the unreason of the natural world. (142)

In fact, Hardoon does fail. The wind ultimately topples
Hardoon's pyramid, and then buries it completely under huge drifts
of dust. And with that, as if having made its point, the wind at last
begins to subside.

In the nature of Hardoon's struggle against the wind, and in his
defeat, lies the symbolic meaning of the cataclysm, and perhaps
also an indication of its true origin in what is a sentient nature or
perhaps an unconscious collective human need. Hardoon is an
embodiment of ego-mind at its most ruthless and arrogant. His
physiognomy, "massive domed forehead, small hard eyes and
callous mouth" (22), emphasizes his over-intellectuality, together
with his lack of vision and of compassion, and events in the story
confirm these traits of his character. His gnome-like deformity, his
habitual dark clothing, and his treacherous, unscrupulous character
recall some evil elf out of Teutonic legend; while his diminutive
physical stature and the repeated comparisons of his face to iron
or granite, together with his very name, serve to suggest an arrested
psychic development, a perverted determination and an infantile
will to omnipotence.

The overthrow of Hardoon's bastion of hubris represents the
victory of nature over human presumption and egocentrism, the
assertion of the irresistible force of "unreason" against the rational,
scientific, technological intelligence and all of its inflated notions
of vanquishing and subduing the natural world. And, although
Hardoon's pyramid is the novel's central emblem of humankind's
grandiosity and impudence, it is far from being the only proud
monument of human achievement that is destroyed by the tempest.
The skycrapers of New York City, London Bridge, Nelson's col-
umn, the Statue of Liberty—all are levelled and swept away by the
wind, as if to serve as a rebuke to an overblown and overbearing
race.

Moreover, although Hardoon may be seen as the supreme exemplar of the egoistic and anthropocentric assumptions of technological civilization, he has no monopoly on such misconceptions. The wind represents a judgment upon a complacent, frivolous, pleasure-seeking society, driven by vanity and sustained by its improvident exploitation of natural resources. The nature of this fundamental cultural blunder is revealed in the general character of the human response to the cataclysm.

> On the whole, people had shown less resourcefulness and flexibility, less foresight, than a wild bird or animal would. Their basic survival instincts had been so dulled, so overlaid by mechanisms designed to serve secondary appetites, that they were totally unable to protect themselves. . . . they were the helpless victims of a deep-rooted optimism about their right to survival, their dominance of the natural order which would guarantee them against everything but their own folly, that they had made gross assumptions about their own superiority.
> Now they were paying the price for this, in truth reaping the whirlwind! (104)

Two details from the novel that seem to suggest larger dimensions of meaning, therefore meriting closer attention, are the manner in which Hardoon's impregnable fortress is overcome, and the general reorganization of human life and society underground that occurs as a consequence of the ravaging wind.

Standing as the concrete manifestation and the very symbol of ego-consciousness and of scientific-technological power, Hardoon's pyramid is ultimately subverted from below by an underground stream that loosens the ground beneath the foundation, opens faults in the surrounding gravel bed, carries away the foundation and finally digs an enormous ravine beneath the left-hand corner of the pyramid into which the unsupported structure topples, impelled by the wind. This undermining "underground spring," (151) the vehicle of the pyramid's destruction and of Hardoon's demise, may be read as a metaphor for the unconscious, which overturns the usurpatory rule of the rational ego-mind, which has, as it were, feet of clay.

In order to escape from the collapsing structures and wind-driven debris on the surface, the people of the earth are forced to take refuge underground. In older towns and cities they find sanctuary in deep cellars, basements, underground tunnels, and in the catacombs. In more modern cities they shelter themselves in the subway and underground systems, in "a sub-world of dark labyrinthine tunnels and shafts" (122), and in "inverted buildings" such as "car parks, underground cinemas, sub-basements and sub-sub-basements" (122–23). Although this movement from the surface to the underground is entirely in accordance with and explicable in terms of the nature of the disaster, it seems also to suggest, in symbolic terms, a retreat from the surface level of consciousness, from the world of the ego, and a corresponding rapprochement with the unconscious.

Ballard's focus in *The Wind from Nowhere* is far less the disaster itself than its effect upon human consciousness. The various characters of the novel respond to the dislocation, danger and distress attendant upon the catastrophe in ways that reveal their essential qualities, their real values and beliefs. On one side of the continuum are the characters of Hardoon and Kroll, representing extremes of ruthless egoism, with the character of Marshall embodying a sort of pragmatic survivorism that is still influenced by moral considerations. Next in sequence is Susan Maitland, a shallow hedonist who succumbs to defeatism at an early stage of the disaster. On the other side of the median are the characters of Dr. Maitland, Commander Lanyon, and Patricia Olsen, all of whom are humane, resolute, and resourceful, preserving courage and compassion throughout the ordeal, even discovering higher values and attaining greater awareness as a result of their trials. The characters of the former group are all destroyed; those of the latter group survive the apocalypse. In the universal tradition of primordial deluges and other mythic catastrophes, the evil are winnowed out while the righteous and worthy are spared to begin another phase of the cosmogonic cycle.

At one point in the novel, Lanyon (one of the very few figures in Ballard's fiction who is unambiguously heroic) recognizes the potential for renewal inherent in the disaster, though in keeping with his conventionally heroic character he equivocates and recants even as he speaks:

> It's curious but until I saw Charlesy lying in that ditch I didn't feel all that concerned. In a way I was almost glad. So much of life in the States—and over here for that matter—could use a strong breath of fresh air. But I realize now that a garbage disposal job of this size rakes away too much of the good along with the bad. (42)

The protagonists of Ballard's subsequent disaster tales, as we shall see, exhibit significantly fewer reservations with regard to the cataclysms with which they are confronted.

It is in Ballard's second novel, *The Drowned World*,[3] that his apocalyptic vision first finds full expression. In distinction to its immediate predecessor, *The Drowned World* possesses not only a tightly-plotted, fast-paced narrative, but also the strange quality of "inner landscape," the resonance of psychic myth. Although these qualities were to some degree already manifest in *The Wind from Nowhere*, they are given significantly more extensive and intensive expression in *The Drowned World*. The narrative of *The Drowned World* is shaped and enriched by patterns of imagery and allusion; indeed, ultimately the novel is to be understood more through its imagery than through its action.

The central imagery of *The Drowned World* is directional: north versus south, with the concomitant associations of up and down, forward and backward. The former direction represents the world as it is perceived by the rationalist, materialist intellect, that is the external world of time and space. The latter represents the unconscious mind, the internal world of timeless transcendent reality. The movement of the book, achieved through the psychic metamorphosis of the novel's protagonist, Dr. Robert Kerans, is from north to south, from rationality to instinct, from the conscious to the unconscious, and from serial time toward cosmic time.

At the beginning of the novel, Karens is still a full participant in the scientific/military expedition of which he has been a member for three years, as it has moved northward across the drowned

European continent. But already the initial signs of Kerans's inner transformation are manifesting themselves: he has begun an "unconscious attempt to sever his links with the base" (8); he realizes that he has reached "a concluding phase of his own life—a northward odyssey" (9); and he begins to discern the emergence of "a personality that had remained latent during his previous adult life" (11). Psychically, Kerans has entered a "zone of transit" (14).

Kerans is not alone in exhibiting signs of psychic disquiet and incipient metamorphosis. Other members of the expedition experience similar symptoms. In particular, the strange dreams of Lieutenant Hardman, his obsession with travelling south and his eventual desertion from the expedition serve to prefigure the transformation to be undergone and the actions to be undertaken by Kerans. There are also indications that the process will ultimately become universal, as humankind begins to undergo "a major metamorphosis" (14) evolving a new psychology.

In this sense, the inundation of the continents of the world by the rising waters of the oceans is an image of the overflowing and overpowering of the individual, conscious, rational intellect, the ego-mind, by the ascendant energies of the unconscious, ultimately by a sort of primordial, transcendent, collective unconscious. As Kerans observes, "the terrestrial and psychic landscapes were now indistinguishable" (74).

The process of psychic metamorphosis, the "descent through archaeopsychic time" (84) upon which Kerans and Hardman, Beatrice and Bodkin have embarked, must inevitably result in physical death, as they recognize, but death is not its goal; that is it is not merely an expression of the death-wish. Indeed, on the contrary, it may be said that the metamorphosis is an expression of the life drive, for it represents the irresistible desire to unite with the very source and ground of all being, as symbolized by the interior sun. The death of the ego and the death of the body are not ends in themselves, but means to the fullest self-realization and to fulfillment in union with ultimate, infinite being.

Bodkin proposes a psycho-biological perspective on the phenomenon of the metamorphosis, explaining it as a descent into the neuronic past of the human mind, a reverse recapitulation of the evolutionary process, "a total reorientation of the personality" (44) provoked by the drastically altered global climate which approximates that of an earlier stage of the biological past. But Bodkin's explanation hardly seems to account for the numinous nature of the experience, and appropriately, this aspect is suggested in a series of similes and metaphors whose common ground is the spiritual: "grail" (46), "Buddhist contemplative" (49), "mandala" (61), "resurrection" (63, 64, 171), and "temple" and "altar" (169–71), among others. The spiritual nature of the psychic metamorphosis is further reinforced by the recurrent Biblical allusions made in the text, particularly those concerning Adam and Eve and Paradise.

Kerans and Beatrice are likened to a new Adam and Eve in quest of a new Eden: a return to a state of consciousness that is beyond space and time. The role of serpent is supplied by the character of Strangman, who like Hardoon in *The Wind from Nowhere* is an embodiment of ego-mind at its most unprincipled and most vicious. It is his demonic power which must be overcome before the return to paradise can be accomplished. Strangman and his crew constitute a cult of death, cruelty, and greed, in every way antithetical to the quest for the archaeopsychic sun and all that it represents. They even attempt to reverse the process of metamorphosis at a material level, draining the lagoon and reclaiming the drowned city. In the end, Kerans succeeds in destroying Strangman and his band, thereby symbolically lifting the malediction that excludes humankind from the paradise of primal, prelapsarian consciousness.

In another parallel, suggesting another archetypal aspect of his character, Kerans becomes a counterpart to the god Neptune, forced by Strangman and his crew to assume that role in their pagan "Feast of Skulls" ceremony. Bound to a throne, Kerans is abused, mocked and nearly murdered as the drunken crew discharge upon him "their fear and hatred of the sea" (37). In keeping with his identification with the god of the sea, Kerans later assists the forces of water—and all that water symbolizes—against the powers of materialism and egotism represented by Strangman, and the powers of rationalism embodied by Riggs, thwarting their combined plans to resist the process of inundation by reclaiming land from the sea.

In addition to the motifs of direction and of water, the cluster of spiritual imagery, and the Biblical and mythological parallels, there are recurring oppositional images in the novel of clocks and of the sun. Clocks, of course, suggest the quantitative, linear, serial time of human convenience and convention, and the realm of the finite: Hardman is instructed to use alarm clocks to counter his dreams of the archaeopsychic sun; Riggs reactivates clocks in the drowned cities. Malfunctioning clocks suggest other cycles and systems of temporal measurement: the timing device on Beatrice's generator runs backwards; the two clock towers of which one is stopped at what is by coincidence "almost exactly the right time" (65) while the other is without hands—symbolizing Kerans's choice between the claims of finite time and those of cosmic time.

The sun, with its corresponding interior archaeopsychic counterpart, represents "Deep Time" (70), "total time" (84), the pulse and rhythm of the cosmos, of eternity. To harmonize and synchronize one's being with cosmic time is to transcend "the single plane of time" with its "negligible claim to reality" (96), and to perceive those who operate on that "tenuous plane" of time as "flat and unreal . . . like intelligent androids" (158).

The southward odyssey, the quest for the sun, represents, in symbolic terms, a quest for absolute, authentic being, for an ontological Eden. The allusions in the text to Adamic man and lost paradise culminate in the closing sentence of the novel, where Kerans is confirmed as "a second Adam searching for the forgotten paradises of the reborn sun" (175). Like the paradise of the Christian faith or those of other spiritual traditions, Ballard's ontological Eden is both primordial and final, a lost, original state of being that can be regained. In the interim between the losing and the recovery, mankind is seen to inhabit a fallen world of fragmented being, and to endure imprisonment in matter and in time and space. Ballard would, in this regard, seem to concur with

William Wordsworth's observation in *The Prelude* that: "Our destiny, our being's heart and home / Is with infinitude, and only there."

The Drowned World establishes two essential patterns that are repeated, deepened and extended in Ballard's subsequent disaster tales. They are set forth with variations in the author's other novels and stories as well. The first of these is that of the self-divided protagonist, most often a doctor or a scientist, who comes to recognize the apocalyptic potential of the particular disaster he is faced with, who perceives it as a metaphor for his own and the general human psychic state, as an interior landscape exteriorized, the fulfillment of an unconscious human desire, and so accepts it, cooperates with it, assists it. Again, it should be noted that this attitude is not nihilistic, nor born of despair or bitter rage; it is grounded in an affirmation of a higher human potential and of the apocalyptic process which is necessary to realize such a potential.

The other pattern is that of the relationship of the protagonist to the other figures in the story. The protagonist usually finds an ally in a female figure who provides guidance and who often acts as an intermediary to and protection from the antagonist. The antagonist is often an ambiguous figure, menacing yet magnetic, a sort of anti-self of the main character, an embodiment of those qualities in himself and in the world that the protagonist opposes and struggles against. Overcoming his antagonist, the main character also resolves his self-dividedness and achieves psychic integration. There are obvious parallels here with the anima and shadow figures of Jungian psychology, and with Carl Jung's theory of the individuation process. In this sense Ballard's fictions are psychic myths, a working out in symbolic terms of our common psychological/spiritual predicament.

Ballard's third novel, *The Drought*,[4] may be seen as the complementary opposite of *The Drowned World*, for despite the diametrical nature of the cataclysms that form the basis of the respective stories, the two novels are mutually reflective, enhancing and underlining each other's meaning through common technical and thematic elements and patterns of imagery. Perhaps the most

central of these is the opposition in both novels of images of sea
and land, of water and earth, with their corresponding symbolic
suggestions of the unconscious and the conscious mind. Where
The Drowned World represented a landscape of the unconscious:
myserious, alluring and fertile; *The Drought* depicts a landscape
of the conscious mind, the ego-mind; arid, desolate and sterile.

The cause of the worldwide drought upon which the novel is
centered is humankind's long-standing pollution of the oceans with
a combination of atomic and industrial wastes, sewage and petro-
leum. Ballard regards such callous and contemptuous abuse of the
natural world as being as much a matter of individual culpability
as it is a collective misdeed. This perspective is emphasized by the
incident early in the novel in which campers empty a chemical
toilet into a river. This slighting and abuse of the natural world has
its inner correspondence in the psyche in the disdain of the rational
mind for the unconscious. The parallels between the outer and
inner dimensions are precise, for in both instances the element
which is disregarded, disparaged, and despised is primary and
vital, essential to the existence of that by which it is rejected and
maltreated.

Just as the wounded oceans of the world withhold, as if by will,
their life-sustaining influence from the land, causing drought, so
also in the novel does the unconscious withhold its beneficial,
nourishing powers from the conscious mind, with the result that
all sense of spiritual communion and of human community is lost,
and the naked ego is given full rein. With the recession of the water,
the protagonist, Dr. Charles Ransom, observes: "Each of them
would soon literally be an island in an archipelago drained of time"
(14). At a later point, Ransom notes the fulfullment of his prophecy,
remarking how "each of them formed a self-contained and discreet
world of his own" (102).

With the advent of the drought every form of human vice thrives,
every predatory and atavistic instinct is given expression: selfishness, suspicion, hostility, fear, revenge, wanton destructiveness,
vicious competitiveness, violence, murder, and cannibalism. This
collapse of all moral restraint, this disintegration of every social

form, is succeeded by a pervading sense of lassitude among the
survivors, a narrowing of vision, a feeling of confinement, a
"gradual attrition of life, the slow reduction of variety and movement" (126). The state of the survivors is repeatedly likened to
limbo; it is a condition in which, as we are told, time has not ceased
but has become "immobilized" (120). This stagnant, static, constricted state of being constitutes an inner prison of profoundest
solitude and silence, the prison of the ego-mind.

The transformation of the landscape during the period of the
drought is an analogue of the transformation that is simultaneously
taking place within the human psyche. The once verdant and fertile
land becomes an arid wasteland, desolate and dead, a wilderness
of dust and sand dunes and half-buried ruins. In the brilliant and
implacable light of the sun there is neither shadow nor color nor
movement. The parallel between the outer and inner worlds is
made explicit in the reflections of Charles Ransom during his
journey inland: "The unvarying light and absence of all movement
made Ransom feel that he was advancing across an inner landscape" (148).

As his portentous name suggests, Dr. Ransom is in search of
redemption, seeking deliverance from the world of time and from
his own consciousness. At the beginning of the novel he feels
strangely "exhilarated" (10) at the progress of the drought, and
"impressed" (34) by what he perceives as the "simple justice" (34)
of the sea's act of retribution. In a metamorphosis parallel to that of
Kerans in *The Drowned World*, a latent self, catalyzed by the
drought, begins to manifest itself in Ransom's psyche. He grows a
"penitential beard" (26) behind which even those closest to him have
difficulty in recognizing him. In contrast to the response of everyone else to the effects of the disaster, he cultivates an acceptance of
"the silence and emptiness" (36) of the new landscape, seeing in it
an opportunity to achieve "absolution in time" (37).

Yet despite this incipient interior metamorphosis, Ransom remains
for much of the novel a self-divided man who resists and evades his
own deepest desires and impulses. The houseboat in which he lives at
the beginning of the drought is an emblem of the state of his psyche:

"a repository of all the talismans of his life . . . a capsule protecting him against the pressures and vacuums of time . . . Here his half-conscious memories of childhood and the past had been isolated and quantified, like the fragments of archaic minerals sealed behind glass cases in museums of geology" (16). It is only by first abandoning this insular, sheltered, static world, and finally through its destruction by fire that Ransom begins to achieve liberation from the burdens of memory and identity.

Ransom's journey to the coast and his ten-year sojourn there constitute a flight from his real desires and from his true identity. At one point during his passage to the sea, he observes the figure of a solitary traveller walking upstream in a dried river bed, and recognizes the inland-bound apparition as "a compass of all the unstated motives that he had been forced to repress" (93). Only after a decade of penance, living as an outcast and a pariah among the salt dunes of the dry ocean beds, does Ransom at last undertake his journey inland, a quest whose direction and distance are metaphors for the traversal of an interior terrain.

The final stages of Ransom's inland journey are characterized by a sense of equanimity and fulfillment. He enters what he describes as "a world of volitional time" (176), a state of consciousness in which he is free of the fixed time of the drought, and in which he achieves liberation from his past and from the imperatives of his exterior identity, attaining "the equation of all emotions and relationships" (183). Beyond this "absolution," the resolution of his prolonged psychic crisis, Ransom seeks to discover or to recover the very source and well-spring of his being, and the promise of grace and rebirth symbolized by the lost river in search of which he sets out, moving further inland. The end of his quest occurs when he finally divests himself of the last remnant of his ego-identity, and experiences the reality of his interior identity and of the world within: "he noticed that he no longer cast any shadow on to the sand, as if he had at last completed his journey across the margins of the inner landscape he had carried in his mind for so many years. The light failed, and the air grew darker. . . . An immense pall of darkness lay over the dunes, as if the whole of the exterior world were losing its existence" (188). Ransom's deliverance is heralded by rainfall, ending the long drought.

A number of overlapping Biblical and literary parallels serve to reinforce and to extend the central imagery of the novel. The most important of these include the stories of Adam and Eve, Noah, and Christ from the Old and New Testaments, Shakespeare's *The Tempest*, and Coleridge's "Rime of the Ancient Mariner." Taking place, as they do, during the drought, and thus divorced from the fecund energies of the unconscious while subject to the distortive influence of the ego-mind, the parallels occur as inferior repetitions or as inversions and travesties of the original stories.

In the manner of the figure of the Ancient Mariner, Ransom violates the bond between humankind and nature by his refusal to sacrifice any of his remaining store of water to revive a dying swan. Like that of the Mariner, Ransom's crime represents an assertion of the ego-mind against the claims of creature-kinship, the bond of man and nature, and thus constitutes a denial of love and compassion. Also in common with the Mariner, Ransom endures a long penance of which drought and thirst are central elements. For both the Ancient Mariner and Ransom the unconscious is the source of ultimate salvation; and for both voyagers absolution is signified by the falling of rain. Finally, both the Mariner and Ransom enact archetypal patterns of guilt and expiation, attaining through their suffering and atonement the status of redemptive figures.

A grotesque parody of *The Tempest* is enacted in the novel by the characters of Quilter, in the role of Caliban; Philip Jordan as Ariel; Richard Lomax as Prospero; and Lomax's sister Miranda as Prospero's daughter of the same name. In the inverted drought version of the story, Caliban, representing the base instincts, triumphs over all the other figures; Ariel forfeits every trace of innocence and ethereality; Miranda becomes depraved and debauched and is reduced at last to breeding Caliban's monstrous offspring; and Prospero is revealed not only as being vindictive and selfish, but also silly and ineffectual, and he is overthrown in the end by Caliban.

Other parody parallels in the novel include that of the story of Noah, his ark, and his daughters, transmogrified by the drought to the Reverend Johnstone, his derelict freighter, and his sleek, over-fed, sinister daughters; together with that of Quilter and Miranda, vicious and corrupt, living among the sterile dunes as a caricature Adam and Eve in an anti-Eden.

A more solemn parallel, though not without its ludicrous aspects, is that of the figure of Jonas enacting the role of a drought Jesus, prophesying the advent of a "new river," and enlisting the local fishermen as his disciples. Serving Jonas in his quest for the new river, the fishermen quite literally become "fishers of men," using their fishing nets to capture and thereafter to impress new converts into their cult. Significantly, Jonas successfully evades the best efforts of the forces of egotism, embodied by Johnstone, Quilter, and Lomax, to capture or kill him. He even survives a parody crucifixion of fatal intent at the hands of his enemies. At the end of the novel Jonas remains at large, still preaching his messianic message of a lost river, by whose secret waters he is himself somehow mysteriously sustained.

Ballard's purpose in employing these and other correspondences as structural devices and as metaphors in *The Drought* would seem to be twofold. By the degree of their divergence, the measure of their disparity from the original models of which they are repetitions, the parallels serve to emphasize the degradation and debasement of human character that occurs under the influence of the (outward and inward) drought. At the same time, they serve to suggest the universality of the issues of *The Drought*: the recurrence of catastrophe (the Fall, the Flood, the Tower of Babel, Sodom and Gommorah, etc.) as a result of pride and vice; and the persistence of occult, redemptive powers in the human spirit.

A final relationship among characters of *The Drought* that should be noted is that of Charles Ransom to Richard Lomax and to Catherine Austen, a configuration with possible Jungian overtones. Lomax represents a sort of anti-self of Ransom: intensely focused upon "the immediate present" (44) and its possibilities for gratification, where Ransom is preoccupied with the past and with absolution in time; Lomax "hard and rapacious" (43) whereas Ransom is essentially considerate and generous; and Lomax indifferent to nature and contemptuous of water ("All that water a mineral I despise, utterly unmalleable . . . ," p. 46), whereas Ransom acknowledges the just claims of the natural world and ultimately sets out in search of the lost sea. Lomax may be seen as another incarnation of the character of Hardoon from *The Wind from Nowhere*, another embodiment of ego-mind. He is described as being "a super-saturation of himself" (44) and as "a plump, grinning Mephistopheles" (47). Consistent with his selfish, satanic nature he also plays the role of the Serpent to Quilter and Miranda's Adam and Eve. Lomax's estate, like Hardoon's pyramid, constitutes a bastion of selfishness, and his destruction of the last reservoir of water in a perverse gesture of proprietorship represents the contradiction inherent in egotism, its essential self-destroying nature.

Catherine Austen seems to personify the positive qualities inherent in the drought, its potential for liberation and renewal, its apocalyptic character. As she remarks to Ransom: "Don't you feel, doctor, that everything is being drained away, all the memories and the stale sentiments?" (19). She seems also to embody certain of the latent and repressed aspects of Ransom's identity, as he recognizes: "there were too many correspondences of character between them, more perhaps than he cared to think" (20). Her association with lions throughout the story suggests her identification with the forces of nature, instinct, and the unconscious. Her survival, like that of Jonas, and the wild freedom of her life with her lions serve to affirm the irrepressibility of the psychic energies of which she is the embodiment.

Ultimately, then, despite its many negative consequences, the drought symbolically accomplishes the overthrow of ego-mind, as represented by Lomax, and the release of unconscious energies, as represented by Catherine Austen and her lions. A corresponding readjustment of psychic forces occurs within Charles Ransom, permitting him at last to complete his inward journey, and to ransom from long captivity his true self.

The Crystal World[5] may be seen as the concluding volume of a tetralogy of disaster novels linked by their common treatment of the themes of psychic integration and transcendence, and by the motif of world cataclysm. The imagery of *The Crystal World* is more explicitly visionary and spiritual in character than that of the preceding volumes, and the theme of apocalypse more fully developed. The cataclysm, which consists of a proliferation of the sub-atomic identity of matter resulting in its crystallization, is cosmic in scope, involving the transfiguration of all life and all matter, and the creation of what is, in the words of St. John the Divine, "a new heaven and a new earth."

The central metaphors of *The Crystal World* are those of light and darkness, of division and unity, and of equilibrium and disequilibrium. The settings and the characters of the novel divide themselves into paired opposites which are associated either with darkness or with light, and which are further distinguished by their possession either of inherent contradictions and conflicts or of poise and integrity. The literal movement of the novel is from the African coastal city of Port Matarre at the mouth of the Matarre estuary, upriver to Mont Royal and into "the crystallized forest"; while the figurative movement (a sort of *Heart of Darkness* in reverse) is from obscurity to clarity, from dissonance to consonance, and from purgatory to paradise.

The main character of the novel, Dr. Edward Sanders, is another self-divided Ballardian protagonist, his psyche locked in conflict between its dark and its light aspects, between his desire to heal and to be healed and his desire to die. Sanders has left the leper hospital of which he is supervising physician, and has come to Port Matarre for reasons which are not entirely clear to him. The ostensible purpose of his journey is to visit his former mistress, Suzanne Clair, and her husband, but at a deeper level he is drawn to Port Matarre by a sense that there he may be able to resolve his psychic crisis: "here at last he might be free of the questions of motive and identity that were bound up with his sense of time and the past" (17).

The terms of Sanders's inner conflict are externalized in the persons whom he encounters during his journey to Port Matarre and during his sojourn there: Ventress, Father Balthus, and Louise Peret. Ventress, with his "bony hand" and his "skull-like face" (13), his white suit, his pistol, his sinister air, and his mortuary remarks, seems to personify death, the death to which Sanders has been so deeply and secretly attracted. Father Balthus, the apostate priest, with his air of imposture, reflects the ambiguity of Sanders's own motives and identity, and embodies Sanders's spiritual yearnings and doubts. Later in the novel, it is suggested that Father Balthus is Sanders's psychic "twin" (123). Louise Peret is the double of Suzanne Clair, but where the latter is identified by Sanders with "the dark side of his psyche" (117), the former represents positive, life-affirming energies.

Sanders's encounter with Louise marks the beginning of a series of events that constitute stages in a process of inner clarification and evolution for him, a process which has significant affinities with what C. G. Jung calls the individuation process, a prolonged series of inner actions and operations by which the psyche is refined, becoming whole. Appropriately, Sanders's first encounter with Louise Peret takes place on the day of the spring equinox, when the forces of darkness and light are of equal strength, and when growth toward the predominance of light begins. Louise catalyzes immediate changes in Sanders, freeing him of his emotional reserve, his "reluctance to involve himself intimately with others" (34), and, more importantly, inspiring him to resist the darkness within himself and causing him to feel new life and hope and a renewed sense of potential.

The next stage of Sanders's psychic development is his encounter with the crystallized forest. Even before he enters the forest he begins to identify himself with it, and when he does enter he is overwhelmed by its surpassing beauty, and profoundly affected by the sense of the numinous that pervades the forest: "he had a curious premonition of hope and longing, as if he were some fugitive Adam chancing upon a forgotten gateway to the forbidden paradise" (71). Sanders also experiences the "rejuvenating" (78) power of the forest, and at one point has a vision of himself as "El Dorado . . . the man of light" (82–83). Yet among the multiple illuminated images of himself that he beholds reflected around himself, he discovers that there still remains "one darker twin" (83). The darkness within his mind and spirit is tenacious.

Despite his fascination with and attraction to the crystalized forest, Sanders persists in perceiving and reacting according to the established categories of thought which he has internalized through his scientific training, and thus fails to comprehend the deeper, truer nature of the phenomenon of crystalization. Returning from the enchanted world of the forest, however, he feels a keen and immediate sense of dejection at the prospect of commonplace reality that now seems to him to be empty and dead. That his return from the forest represents a retreat from the process of psychic evolution in which he is engaged is signalled by Sanders's change of costume: he appropriates the suit of a deceased patient at the Mont Royal Clinic, dressing himself in "dead man's clothes" (116) whose "darker material seemed more appropriate for this nether world" (117). Seeing him thus attired, Louise Peret is prompted to comment: "I almost didn't recognize you, Edward. This suit, it's like a disguise" (120).

As a result of his sojourn in the crystallized zones Sanders has learned to recognize the nature of his inner division, and to accept the necessity to strive toward some form of psychic harmony: "there's a dark side of the psyche, and . . . all one can do is find the other face and try to reconcile the two—it's happening out there in the forest" (123). Impelled by his desire for such reconciliation, Sanders re-enters the forest, becomes partly crystallized, attains communion with his "twin," Father Balthus, who has at last achieved his own psychic clarification. But again Sanders resists the imperatives of the process, and departs from the forest once more. As Ventress remarks to Sanders: "You aren't ready to come here yet" (144).

Through this second sojourn, however, Sanders is deeply altered. The true origins and meaning of the catacylsm-by-crystalization are now clear to him: "it's obvious to me now that its origins are more than physical" (154). He perceives the redintegrative, redemptive potential of the phenomenon, and he is at last capable of accepting the sacrifice that must be made in order to attain the vital grace and ultimate benediction conferred by the process: "There the transfiguration of all living and inanimate forms occurs before our eyes, the gift of immortality a direct consequence of the surrender by each of us of our physical and temporal identities" (154). At the conclusion of the novel Sanders has again embarked upon a journey upriver to the forest of Mont Royal, in quest of the "final resolution" (158) of psychic disequilibrium that is to be found only within the crystal world.

The ambient conflict in *The Crystal World*, of which Sanders's psychic crisis is a reflection, is that of two levels or realms of reality: the world of commonplace reality with its familiar physical laws; and the world within the "affected zones" of the earth, the crystal world. The world of everyday reality, the world as we know it, is characterized in the novel as a realm of division and conflict, of confusion and doubt, and of time and death. Port Matarre, which serves in the story as the symbol of ordinary reality, is compared to a "necropolis" (9), and is further likened to "purgatory" (27, 74). It is a realm of shadow and darkness, pervaded by a sense of unease and foreboding. When Sanders returns from his first sojourn in the crystallized forest he is dismayed to perceive quotidian reality as "inert and empty . . . a spent world," a world that seems to him flat, drab, and unreal.

In contrast to this world, the crystal world is paradisical, a realm of Platonic perfection. It is the true, bright, original image of which our world is but "a faded reflection" (74). In the crystal world there is beauty, harmony, and unity. There, there is no darkness or division but all is illuminated, reconciled, and transfigured. The zones constitute a world beyond time, as evidenced by the metamorphosis of Sanders's wristwatch. When inside the zone: "spurs of crystal grew from the dial . . . imprisoning the hands within a medallion of moonstone" (103); while once outside the zone: "The last of the crystals on the dial of the wristwatch gave out their light and faded, and with a sudden movement the hands began to turn" (107).

For the characters of Radek, Thorensen, Serena, Suzanne Clair, and the lepers, the crystallized zone represents surcease from sickness and sorrow, and ultimate wholeness and fulfillment. For the apostate Father Balthus the zone provides final faith and absolute conviction: "the body of Christ is with us everywhere here—" (147). For Sanders the crystal world offers true identity. After his second visit to the zone Sanders feels himself quite alien and but a half-hearted participant in the world of commonplace reality: "his real identity still moved through the forests of Mont Royal. . . . he felt like the empty projection of a self that still wandered through the forest" (156–57).

The terms and images in which the crystal world is depicted are essentially spiritual in character: "paradise" (71, 74, 150), "the New Jerusalem" (125), "a vision materalized from St. John the Divine" (153), "the final celebration of the Eucharist of Christ's body . . . the last marriage of space and time" (148). Moreover, the physical characteristics of the crystal world, its exquisite beauty, its elaborate, intricate architectures and its ubiquitous self-luminous gems possess close affinities with the archetypal paradises of the visionary experience and with the heavens, fairylands, and Other Worlds of folklore and spiritual tradition.[6] The crystal world represents Ballard's most compelling and most fully-realized "ontological Eden," and as such constitutes an appropriate concluding image to his apocalyptic tetralogy.

Ballard's four novels of disaster compose a fourfold "arraignment of the finite," an indictment of the limitations placed upon consciousness by ego-mind, rationalism, materialism and linear time. The four novels affirm, on the other hand, the unconscious and its imperatives, in particular the urge for transcendence. The novels also possess common structural-symbolic patterns according to which those characters embodying ego-mind are ultimately overthrown or undone. The protagonists of the separate stories attain rapport with anima figures and undergo metamorphoses in the course of which their latent identities are realized, identities whose fullest elaboration necessitates the relinquishing of the physical, temporal, conscious self.

Another concomitant pattern uniting the four novels is that of a radical transformation of the earth's appearance in such a manner that it comes to resemble and to correspond to a preexistent inner landscape, a deep and potent image in the collective human psyche which may have the character of penance and retribution, or of paradise and transcendence.

Ballard's novels of cataclysm represent a response and a rebuke to the scientific-materialist orientation of our age, and to the meretriciousness and rapaciousness of our technological-commercial culture. They further serve to awaken our consciousness to a new awareness of our identities, interpreting our equivocal and unsuspected motives, and examining the secret recesses of our psyches. And, finally, they propose a reconsideration of the nature of reality itself.

Technological Tartarus: *The Atrocity Exhibition, Crash, Concrete Island, High Rise*

The following four books to be discussed in this section may be said to constitute a sort of diagnosis and prognosis of the malady afflicting modern consciousness. The first book is largely concerned with the etiology and the symptoms of the disorder; the following three books weigh the prospects of recovery and consider various means of treatment.

The first of these books, *The Atrocity Exhibition*,[1] is neither a novel nor a collection of short stories, but a series of interrelated vignettes which possess common themes, images, and characters. The separate sections of the book, numbered and titled, consist, in turn, of sequences of individually titled paragraphs, the whole constituting an inventory of signs, indices, and instances as evidence toward the identification of a mental, moral, metaphysical illness. The narrative is discontinuous and non-linear; the style combines the clinical and the lyrical. The book is generally regarded as Ballard's most experimental and is likewise considered to be his least accessible.

Certainly the fragmented form and the dense writing make demands upon the patience and the attention of the reader, but the book rewards close reading, offering insights into contemporary reality which could be communicated fully and accurately only by means of such stylistic techniques and devices as the author employs. Moreover, the book possesses numerous points of continuity with Ballard's previous writing, including character names, phrases, and motifs, which serve as markers and signposts to the reader already familiar with Ballard's work. At the same time, these points of continuity may also in their present context serve to illuminate previous works by the author, while other elements in the book prefigure subsequent works. In this manner, *The Atrocity Exhibition* may be seen to be at the center of Ballard's oeuvre, and to represent a grammar of the themes and images of his work.

A dominant and encompassing theme of *The Atrocity Exhibition* is that of the emotional and spiritual sterility of contemporary Western culture, its loss of vitality and of direction. This theme is manifest in the book's recurrent imagery of bare and forbidding urban settings and of a landscape of physical deterioration, and is further evinced in the profound sense of estrangement, of ennui and despair that distinguishes the lives of the inhabitants of this present-day dystopia, and in the mechanistic, dehumanized character of their interpersonal relationships.

The world of *The Atrocity Exhibition* is depicted in terms of a wasteland and an inferno. It is a landscape of desolation and dereliction: deserted, dilapidated buildings, waste grounds, concrete causeways, freeways, underpasses, billboards, anonymous apartment blocks and endless suburbs, multi-story car parks and spectral petrochemical plants, and everything broken or cracked, corroded, tattered or rusty, everywhere littered with debris; the natural landscape obscured, ravaged, or exhausted. Ballard names this Dantesque zone "the suburbs of Hell" (9, 16).

The outer landscape depicted in *The Atrocity Exhibition* represents, as in previous works by Ballard, the externalization of an inner landscape, the reflection of internal barrenness and devastation. The human body here also becomes a landscape, its scars, bruises, injuries, and disfigurations—recurrent images in the book—serving as the outward and visible signs of a deeper woundedness. The living death of the inhabitants of Ballard's inferno is personified in the character of Traven who, as the result of an airplane disaster, "was dead for about two minutes" on the operating table. As a consequence, "something is missing, something that vanished during the short period of his death. Perhaps his soul, the capacity to achieve a state of grace" (37). Traven's condition is emblematic of that of his fellow residents of "the suburbs of Hell," a death-in-life, a state of estrangement from the sources of true being.

A direct extension of such a condition of mind and spirit is the degradation of human relationships that occurs in *The Atrocity Exhibition*. The intermittence of the mannequin motif in the text suggests the reduction of human individuals to objects, anonymous units to be exploited without emotion or accountability. Mannequins and persons, the two having become virtually interchangeable in the world of *The Atrocity Exhibition*, are repeatedly utilized as victims in elaborately staged private scenarios or psychodramas. The equation of human and mannequin is further evidenced in Talbot's reflections upon his mistress: "Already she had the texture of a rubber mannequin, fitted with explicit vents, an obscene masturbatory appliance" (19).

Accordingly, sexuality in the infernal system of *The Atrocity Exhibition* has become purely "conceptual" (56, 63) in nature, an abstract act devoid of tenderness or sensuality. The cultivation of sexual perversions has become necessary in order to provoke any real erotic passion, and even this stratagem proves to be inadequate, requiring the invention of new perversions as the familiar ones lose their potency. As the character of Karen Novotny observes: "these activities were evidence of an ever widening despair, a deliberate summoning of the random and the grotesque" (77). The ultimate perversion and the highest degree of despair, though, are manifest in the substitution of violence and death for the positive and creative energies of eroticism and love. This tendency, evident throughout the book, culminates in the section titled "The Generations of America," which parodies the biblical text of the generations of the sons of Noah in the Book of Genesis, replacing the biblical word "begot" with the word "shot." This simple but all-significant substitution of verbs—signifying the supplanting of our deepest creative urges with acts of destruction—is the final measure of our fallen condition.

Another central theme of *The Atrocity Exhibition* is its exploration of the latent meaning of the landscapes and artifacts of our culture and our daily lives in the late twentieth century: films, the media, nuclear armament, advertising, contemporary urban architecture, political figures, automobiles—all are interpreted in terms of their concealed significance, their status as evidence of our real motives and values. Dr. Nathan, who functions in the book in a fashion similar to that of the chorus in Greek tragedy—interpreting, elucidating the motives of the characters and the significance of events in the text—remarks that "it is clear that Freud's classic distinction between the manifest and latent content of the inner world of the psyche now has to be applied to the outer world of reality" (99). The book itself represents such an inquiry, uncovering the curious ambiguities of violence and desire that constitute the substratum of the everyday reality of our era.

The latent content of the particular aspects of reality scrutinized in *The Atrocity Exhibition* seems most often to contradict the manifest content. Thus, a military weapons range reveals itself as a model of the body and face of the actress Elizabeth Taylor, suggesting the latent erotic implications of firearms and weaponry. Apparently functional architecture such as that of a multi-story car park proves also to embody erotic impulses, replicating in its canted floors aspects of female anatomy. The phenomenon of the automobile crash is shown to represent "a fertilizing rather than a destructive event—a liberation of sexual energy" (23), while the unconscious role of thermonuclear weapons is seen to be a collective human desire to achieve "the total fusion and nondifferentiation of all matter" (34).

Common to these and other instances of the latent meaning of external reality as proposed in *The Atrocity Exhibition* is the sense that our deepest impulses are creative, and that despite their being suppressed, thwarted, and perverted by forces inherent in our selves, in our society, and in the nature of reality itself, they remain potent, perpetually subversive, seeking expression in whatever form they may take, making our motives and our identities equivocal.

The theme of transcendence is again treated in *The Atrocity Exhibition*, together with the themes of psychic integration and apocalypse with which it is often closely allied. The composite protagonist of the book—alternately named Travis, Talbot, Traven, Tallis, Trabert, Talbert, Travers—is distinguished by the "failure of his psyche to accept the fact of its own consciousness" (11) and by his revolt against "the very facts of time and space" (36). Rejecting "the rigid and unyielding structures of his own consciousness" (22), T. (as I shall call him) is engaged in a search for an original and lost symmetry, a mode of being beyond the phenomenological universe.

As one simile in the text images it, it is as if T. is "trying to force a corridor to the sun" (24). His method of forcing a corridor to a new clarity is self-induced psychosis, a journey into personal apocalypse. (Again, there is a parallel here to Rimbaud's "systematic derangement of the senses" whose aim was to attain "a new lucidity" and to become "a seer.") Through the acting out of his obsessions and the cultivation of his compulsions, T. proposes to subvert his conscious identity and thereby to redeem his psyche from the "nightmarish excresence" (57) and the "biomorphic horror" (77) of consciousness trapped in matter in a universe of time and space. Unlike the quests of protagonists in Ballard's other works, however, T.'s search for an ontological Eden remains unresolved.

Simultaneous with T.'s endeavor to achieve a higher sanity by going mad, another complementary process is taking place within his psyche. T. mysteriously attracts or perhaps conjures two tutelary figures who become his companions: a bomber pilot and a beautiful young woman disfigured by radiation burns. He senses that the role of "these strange twins" is that of "couriers from the unconscious" (9). The two figures seem to objectify conflicting energies in T.'s psyche, that of Eros and that of Thanatos, the former having been subjugated and injured by the latter. The pilot and the young woman seem also to have their counterparts in or to blend into or merge with the characters of Catherine Austen and Karen Novotny and the character of Vaughan. However, the process of psychic integration that is suggested by T.'s relationship to these figures, though it is further developed, is not brought to any clear or final resolution in the book.

Although the quest of the protagonist to recover lost symmetry of consciousness and to achieve true identity remains unresolved, the possibility at least of its ultimate realization is suggested by two groups of images that recur throughout the book: imagery drawn from mathematics, especially geometry—modulus, angle, plane, dimension, etc.—and imagery drawn from and allusions to surrealism—Lautréamont, Matta, Bellmer, Tanguy, Ernst, et al. Though seemingly incongruous, both clusters of imagery possess a common ground in what may be seen as a shared metaphysic: their foundation in patterns of meaning inherent in and yet transcending the phenomenological world. Both groups of images serve in the text to suggest an absolute reality beyond material, temporal reality, and a mode of being that transcends the realm of the senses and of ego-consciousness.

The novel *Crash*[2] is a direct extension of certain ideas from *The Atrocity Exhibition* concerning the relationships among violence, eroticism, technology, and transcendence. Related to *The Atrocity Exhibition* by common scenes, characters, and motifs, *Crash* carries to their logical, if profoundly disturbing, conclusion notions introduced in the former book. *Crash* may be seen as an inquiry into the ambiguities of our modern "machine landscape" (46), our technological culture. The book employs the automobile as a symbol of technology in order to raise questions regarding the latent motives behind and the true nature of all technology: whether it suppresses and degrades, diverts and perverts our spiritual aspirations, our appetites for the sublime and the infinite, or whether, in fact, it may have been (unconsciously, inadvertently) designed precisely to further those aspirations and appetites; whether technology serves ends which are subversive to its manifest intentions and apparent functions; whether, in spite of itself, technology also constitutes an arraignment of the finite.

Crash proposes the automobile collision as a contemporary expression of the same impulse that informs ancient fertility rites involving human sacrifice, as a supreme erotic act, and as a catalyst to mystical experience and transcendence. The true purpose of the automobile is thus not a means of transportation but a vehicle of our deepest desires; its real end and object not efficiency and convenience of movement, but sexual consummation, spiritual affirmation, ritual mutilation, sacrifice, self-immolation, and a shamanistic release of fertilizing, creative energy into the physical world and the world of the spirit. In this way the ultramodern is seen to be in reality no more than a complex manifestation of the primordial.

Crash is written as a first-person narrative, told by a character named Ballard, who at the chronological beginning of his story is a conventional, middle-aged, urban professional. Involved on his way home from work one afternoon in an automobile collision in which a passenger in the other car is fatally injured, Ballard himself receives only minor injuries, but the event marks for him the inception of a process of psychic metamorphosis that alters all his values and perspectives, and transforms his character and his mode of life. Already while still pinned in the wreckage of his car, Ballard's perception of the world begins to change as he sees patterns made by the wreckage of his automobile "repeated" (22) in the persons and objects around him; and notes, at the same time, the sexual and ritual elements of the event and its participants.

The minor wounds which Ballard sustains in the collision represent insignia of his rite of passage from the world of quotidian reality to a region of mysterious and compelling obsessions. He becomes aware of the emergence of a "new character" within him, and compares his altered state of consciousness to that of "someone in a science-fiction film, stepping out of his capsule after an immense inward journey on to the overlit soil of an unfamiliar planet" (32). Characteristic of Ballard's emergent personality is a new intensity and range of erotic response, together with an impassioned interest in every aspect and extension of the automobile. Driven home from the hospital, he is exhilarated to experience the "enchanted domain" (41) of the freeway, feeling keen excitement at the sight of cars in motion. Returning to his familiar neighborhood, Ballard now perceives it as trivial, inert, and essentially unreal, possessing none of the "keys to the borders of identity" (42) whose presence he senses in automobiles and on the motorways.

Ballard's inner metamorphosis proceeds by stages as he becomes increasingly fascinated with the erotic potentials of the automobile and increasingly attracted by the prospect of his own eventual death in a collision. The partners with whom he engages in sexual intercourse during the period following his accident may be seen as increments on an ascending scale of obsession. With each partner—Renata, Helen Remington, Gabrielle, Vaughan—Ballard exceeds an inner boundary, triumphs over a sexual inhibition or convention and achieves a higher degree of libidinal liberation. Each collision of flesh is a rehearsal for the apocalyptic car crash for which he yearns so devoutly; each sexual act represents a step closer to the "ultimate and yet undreamt of sexual union" (27), the transcendent erotic consummation toward which he aspires. At the conclusion of the narrative he is fully committed to his death-in-orgasm collision. At last, in the wake of Vaughan's death, having forsaken all resistance, Ballard surrenders himself to the "logic and beauty" of such a death: "Already I knew that I was designing the elements of my own car crash (171).

The metamorphosis of the narrator from ordinary, complacent urban citizen and commonplace, contemporary materialist-hedonist to obsessed, self-immolating erotic-mystic is paralleled by similar transformations of other characters in the story. Both Helen Remington and Gabrielle undergo radical personality changes corresponding to those of the narrator as a result of their automobile accidents. Gabrielle's transformation is meticulously documented in Vaughan's photographic record of her accident and its aftermath: "The first photographs of her lying in the crashed car showed a conventional young woman whose symmetrical face and unstretched skin spelled out the whole economy of a cozy and passive life. . . ." But the accident shatters her superficial identity and smashes all of her socially-conditioned reflexes to life even as it demolishes the flimsy fiberglass body of her vehicle: "The crushed body of the sports car had turned her into a creature of free and perverse sexuality, releasing within its twisted bulkheads and leaking engine coolant all the deviant possibilities of her sex" (79). Gabrielle's crippling accident is imaged as a baptism and a rebirth, as an erotic ordeal that rescues her from "an increasingly abstracted despair," and as a traumatic catalylst for the emergence of "a second personality" and the emancipation of "the hidden faces of her psyche" (78).

The characters Seagrave and Vaughan are both parallels to and forerunners of the narrator, their fixations and psychic developments reflecting his own, and their deliberate deaths in car collisions prefiguring his projected crash. Vaughan, in particular, personifies the car-sex-death equation of the novel. The "nightmare angel of the expressways" (68), he embodies more than any other character in the novel the ambiguities of violence and desire, and the paradoxical amalgam of demonic and redemptive energies that inform the story.

The twin themes of apocalypse and transcendence are central to *Crash*. The individual collisions undergone or undertaken by the narrator, by Vaughan, and the other characters of the story are seen as portents of and rehearsals for an imminent "autogeddon" (43, 85), an ultimate, simultaneous, world-wide orgy of annihilation by automobile. As Ballard observes: "When we've all rehearsed our separate parts the real thing will begin" (43). The altered consciousness of each crash veteran serves to affect and alter other drivers, or as Ballard images it, the wounds of each crash victim become beacons "tuned to a series of beckoning transmitters, carrying the signals . . . which would unlock this immense stasis and free these drivers for the real destinations set for their vehicles" (46). The source of these transmitters would seem to be the collective unconscious of modern humankind, and the text of the message: destruction and deliverance.

The imagery by which the transcendent character of the experience of automobile collision is conveyed in the novel is that of light and luminosity, and of ascension or flight. Radiance, brilliance, illumination, gleamings, glimmerings, shinings, flashings, sheens, glows, nimbuses, and coronas are recurrent throughout the text in conjunction with the raptures of the crash. Images of rainbows and of jewels and crystal are also prominent in the same connection. Vaughan's face, for example, is "lit by broken rainbows" (12) after one of his collisions, while an injured woman driver is described as having "fragments of the tinted windshield set in her forehead like jewels" (14). There are rainbows of urine and of wounds (22, 23, 26) in the wake of collisions, and the "crystal" of broken safety glass (48), while the instrument panel is imaged as "a jewelled grotto" (66). When Seagrave kills himself in his carefully orchestrated sex-death collision, he is "covered with shattered safety glass, as if his body were already crystallizing, at last excaping out of this uneasy set of dimensions into a more beautiful universe" (142).

Clearly, such imagery resonates with that of earlier Ballard paradises, especially that of *The Crystal World*, and serves here to suggest the transporting, transfiguring nature of the crash experience. The imagery of light unites with recurrent religious imagery—"angel" (67), "baptized" (78), "sermon" (121), "eucharist" (121), "saintly relic" (144), "altarpieces" (153)—to culminate in the narrator's apocalyptic LSD-induced vision of earthly traffic transformed into a radiant "metallized Elysium," with "An armada of angelic creatures" (152) landing on the roads and motorways. In the same manner as the highways, as we are told, were "unknowingly" (152) constructed to receive these heavenly beings, so the automobile was unknowingly designed to be an instrument for the attainment of mystical rapture and ultimate reality.

Imagery of ascension and flight is also employed to express the transcendent character of the car crash. The freeway is depicted as resembling "a secret airstrip from which mysterious machines would take off into a metallized sky" (19); automobiles are repeatedly described as possessing wings, even "wings of fire" (159), whose purpose is "our coming passage to heaven" (160). Vaughan's last crash is seen by the narrator as an effort "to launch himself into the sky" (169); and Vaughan's spirit is depicted as surviving in the form of a "glass aeroplane" (19) that traverses in angelic benediction the skies above our bored, worn, depleted world.

The car-crash compulsion, like the advent of the wind from nowhere, the drought, the rising waters of *The Drowned World*, or the crystallization process, constitutes a willed catastrophe, an apocalypse deeply desired by the unconscious. The crash represents an act of transcendence, the gateway to an ontological Eden.

Another dimension of meaning of the automobile collision as depicted in *Crash* is its secret role as a ritual of sacrifice and fertility. This latent meaning is understood at an unconscious level by the hundreds of spectators who are attracted to the crash sites of the novel, drawn by the vicarious enactment of "the secret formulas" (18) of their own minds and lives. The initiates or adepts of the car crash, such as the narrator, Vaughan, Seagrave, Gabrielle, and others, represent sacrificial victims in whose ritual acts of sex and violence vital energies are released that purge and nourish the human community in a manner parallel to the practices of self-wounding, self-mutilating cults of the primitive (i.e. non-technological) world. In this regard, Vaughan's semen is described as having "bathed" the landscape, and as "irrigating" the lives of its inhabitants (146), while the narrator proposes that the "translation" or ritualization of the deaths and injuries of traffic casualties into acts of sexuality represents "the only way of re-invigorating those wounded and dying victims" (146). Later, the narrator proclaims that "In our wounds we celebrated the rebirth of the traffic-slain dead, . . . [and] . . . of the millions yet to die" (155). After Vaughan's death, the narrator performs an act of "ritual love" (170) with his wife in Vaughan's car, anointing the deathcar with his semen, celebrating the dissemination throughout the world of Vaughan's potent, fructifying, redemptive energies:

> Meanwhile the traffic moves in an unceasing flow along the flyover. The aircraft rise from the runways of the airport, carrying the remnants of Vaughan's semen to the instrument panels and radiator grilles of a thousand crashing cars, the leg stances of a million passengers. (171)

Crash may be read as an extreme metaphor for the spiritual crisis of our culture. Clearly, the book is descriptive and not prescriptive, articulating a vision of the metaphysical void in which we exist and of the desperate responses our unconscious minds may make to resist the desacralization of life effected through the triumph of rationality and science. Although the book depicts actions and attitudes abhorrent to our moral sense, it may also be read as an affirmation of the survival and the persistence of forces in the psyche that seek to redeem us from the sterility and futility of our lives in the world and from the prison of material, temporal existence, from the finite universe.

The author has himself acknowledged the ambiguities implicit in *Crash*:

> one needs to dismantle that *smothering conventional reality* that wraps itself around us . . . and of course violent acts of various kinds, whether they're car crashes or serious illnesses or any sort of trauma, do have that sort of liberating effect. . . . When I was writing *Crash* I did a fair amount of research, particularly in this book called *Crash Injuries*, a medical textbook full of the most gruesome photographs . . . all one's pity goes out to these tragically mutilated people. . . . But at the same time, one cannot help one's imagination being touched by these people who, if at enormous price, have nonetheless broken through the skin of reality and convention around us . . . and who have in a sense achieved—become— mythological beings in a way that is only attainable through these brutal and violent acts. One can transcend the self, sadly, in ways which are in themselves rather to be avoided.[3]

The car crash as symbolic act serves as a transitional image between *Crash* and Ballard's next novel, *Concrete Island.*[4] *Concrete Island* opens with a crash as the automobile driven by the protagonist, Robert Maitland, leaves the motorway while travelling at high speed, due to the blow-out of a front tire with attendant loss of driver control. The vehicle plunges down the embankment and comes to rest at last on a small traffic island "some two hundred yards long and triangular in shape, that lay in the waste ground between three converging motorway routes" (10). Despite his persistent efforts to escape from the island and return to his comfortable, affluent life, Maitland remains marooned on the island for the length of the novel.

Concrete Island is an allegory of psychic integration achieved through catastrophe. Robert Maitland is a self-divided, self-estranged man who has lost contact with his deeper being, and who is only marginally aware of so being and of having so done. However, as he begins to suspect almost immediately following his crash and his arrival on the island, and as he later accepts, he has deliberately—though unconsciously—arranged his crash, created his situation willfully though without conscious premeditation. The conflict of the story is thus less between Maitland and his new environment than between Maitland and his unconscoius mind.

The pattern of Maitland's conflict with his unknown self is that of unwilling confrontation, stubborn resistance, gradual acceptance, and finally integration. This pattern is paralleled in his relation to the island itself, which represents an objectification of his unconscious; and, with some variation, the pattern may also be seen in his relationship to the two inhabitants of the island, Proctor and Jane Sheppard, who embody aspects of his latent identity.

At the instant of the blow-out of the front tire of his automobile that is the cause of the crash, we are told that "The exploding air reflected from the concrete parapet seemed to detonate inside Robert Maitland's skull" (7). In a metaphoric sense an explosion does occur within Maitland's head at this moment: his familiar reality and his familiar identity are being exploded, collapsed like the tire of his car. The first indication that Maitland has been altered by his sudden and violent passage "Through the Crash Barrier," as the chapter title ambiguously images his experience, is the reflection of his face in the rear-view mirror immediately after the accident, his familiar features transformed to resemble those of "a psychotic twin brother" (8). Shortly thereafter Maitland notes his "distorted reflection" on the polished surface of his car: his figure "warped" and his face fixed with "a madman's grimace" (12). His subsequent erratic, euphoric behavior on the motorway as he attempts to wave down one of the passing cars is a further evidence of an emergent identity, but he manages to "rally all his powers of self-control" (17) and thus to sustain for a little while longer his accustomed self. By the afternoon of his second day on the island, however, Maitland is again behaving like "an exultant madman" while his clothes, the outward sign of his social identity, now cling to him "like a dead animal" (34). At the same time, Maitland's increasingly tramp-like appearance and his being mistaken for a tramp by passing drivers (14, 27, 40) prefigure his later identity with his psychic counterpart, the tramp-acrobat, Proctor.

Maitland's inner metamorphosis unfolds despite his determined tactics of resistance, which include talking aloud to himself as "a self-identification signal" (23) and, grown increasingly desperate, shouting his own name again and again, "trying to identify himself" (47). After four days on the island Maitland has already begun to forget his family, his mistress, and his job; after an additional two or three days it is only with "a deliberate effort" (104) that he can recall his former life. In the meantime, Maitland is discovering and cultivating sources of inner power and energy previously dormant, and achieving new confidence and control. In the end, he attains a new purposefulness and determination, a resolution of his self-dividedness, and a new sense of identity. Maitland's newly constructed shelter on the island, built from discarded sections of car bodies and named by him "the pavillion of doors" (116), symbolizes his new receptivity to life, his awareness of life's many possibilities, its many entrances and means of access.

Maitland's changing perspective on his life and identity is also reflected in his growing recognition of the real nature of the island and of his relation to it. In the beginning, just after his crash, the island represents to him no more than an inconvenience, an interruption of his life. Soon after, he begins to perceive it as a threat: "If you don't look out you'll be beached here forever" (25). At this point he still regards the island with disdain, remarking on its "meaningless soil" (25). After the repeated failure of his attempts to escape from the island, however, Maitland conceives a sort of grudging respect for the island, perceiving it in terms of a personal challenge, vowing to meet it "on equal terms" (41) and even to "dominate" (45) it. The soil is no longer meaningless to him but appreciated for its exemplary powers of endurance: "The resilience of this coarse grass was a model of behavior and survival" (43).

Slowly, as he comes to know the topography of the island and to acquaint himself with its secrets and mysteries, Maitland begins to identify the island with himself, recognizing in it "an exact model of his head" (51), and declaring "I am the island" (52, 93). At the same time he begins to perceive the island as more extensive than he had first judged it to be: "The island seemed larger and more contoured . . ." (74), and, "The embankments seemed further away than he remembered them, slowly receding from him on all sides. By contrast the island appeared far larger . . . " (86). This altered sense of proportion suggests the changes that are occurring in Maitland's sense of values and priorities: his former reality and his former identity are now of diminished appeal and importance to him. Indeed, at last, he feels "no real need to leave the island" (126), though he retains his intention of doing so.

The nature and significance of the island can best be understood through a consideration of its salient characteristics, its powers and properties, and of the imagery in terms of which it is described. The island comprises an abandoned graveyard, a ruined cinema, World War II air raid shelters, the remains of a civil defense post, and the foundations of razed Edwardian houses, together with their overgrown gardens. Perhaps the most important feature of the island is that it is characterized as being sentient and animate, "an immense green creature" (50) whose vegetation responds to Maitland according to his intentions, and, in turn, communicates its own intentions to him: waking him, beckoning him, restraining him, guiding him, greeting him, rebuking him. Ultimately, Maitland learns to read the grass, sensing its vibrations with his hands. The grass is also repeatedly imaged as an ocean or a sea (see, for example, pp. 20, 30, 31, 54, 90, among many others)—imagery which traditionally, and in Ballard's previous work, has been used to suggest the unconscious.

For Maitland the island corresponds to the image of a lost childhood paradise which has haunted him in his adult life, and it evokes actual childhood memories as well. One notable effect of the island upon Maitland is to cause him to regain something of his childhood self. Despite his injuries, his misfortunes, and frustrations, Maitland taps the roof of his car "with almost child-like humour" (45) on the morning of his second day on the island. Subsequently, he is compared to "a child at play" (45), and his sodden jacket is likened to "a child's football gear" (47). His body is described as "more and more beginning to resemble that of his younger self" (66), and he is fed "child's food" (74) by Jane Sheppard, who babies him and identifies him with her lost child. Thus, as Maitland recognizes, "His movement across this forgotten terrain was a journey not merely through the island's past but through his own" (51).

Another effect of the island upon Maitland is that of a reorientation of his temporal sense. From the instant of his crash and for several days thereafter, Maitland makes frequent and precise notations of time. Even after the theft of his wristwatch by Proctor, he continues to estimate time, judging the hour by the direction and intensity of the passing traffic and by the angle of the sun. At last, though, he begins to neglect such measurements, and on his seventh or eighth day on the island he realizes without regret "that he had forgotten what day it was—Wednesday, or perhaps Friday" (112). Forsaking quantitative time, Maitland becomes responsive to the immediate stimuli of the diurnal cycle: the morning and the evening dew, the movement of shadows across the terrain, the quality of the light, the warmth or coolness of the air.

Clearly, the island represents an embodiment of the unconscious: a fluid, timeless zone, a lost paradise, a region of wild flora, forgotten ruins, and abandoned objects, a place of danger and of fertile mystery. Maitland is renewed by contact with the island and its potent, primal forces, achieving a new identity and a higher awareness, and even, despite his deprivations, developing new physical strength "as if the unseen powers of his body had begun to discharge their long-stored energies" (125). In this manner, Maitland's unconsciously willed crash constitutes a catastrophe which at a personal level is a parallel to the cataclysms of the author's other disaster novels. The purpose of these catastrophes, great or small, is manifestly the same: "to dismantle that *smothering conventional reality* that wraps itself around us."

The role of the island's two inhabitants, Proctor and Jane, as embodiments of unconscious energies and as externalizations of aspects of Maitland's own psyche, may be most fully apprehended in the context of the implicit parallels between *Concrete Island* and Shakespeare's *The Tempest*. In Ballard's contemporary version of the story each character plays a double role. Maitland enacts the roles of both Prospero and his usurping brother Antonio. Just as Prospero raises the tempest that wrecks Antonio upon the island, Maitland's unconscious mind, his latent self, wills the crash that brings his usurping ego-identity, his superficial self, to the traffic island. And, as is the case with Prospero and Antonio, where the latter renounces his unlawfully acquired power and position and is reconciled with the brother whom he has wronged and driven into exile, so the superficial Maitland yields his predominance to the latent Maitland who has endured interior exile for so many years, and the two are reconciled as one identity.

Jane Sheppard plays the roles of the witch Sycorax, the original ruler of the island before the arrival of Prospero and of Miranda, Prospero's lovely and innocent daughter. Jane's double role is reflected in her appearance, "like a down-at-heel witch" (61) whose "open and child-like face" bears an expression of "naive corruption" (73); and in her conduct as well, which is "a mixture of warmth and aggressiveness" (72) and ingenuousness and deviousness. Her attitude toward Maitland varies from "tenderness and good humour to sudden vengeful anger" (81), as she alternately rescues and poisons him, makes love to him and strikes and taunts him, helps him and plots against him. Jane's equivocal nature would seem to identify her with the anima figure of Jungian psychology, which possesses two aspects, benevolent and malefic, comprehending both the role of guide and nurturer as well as that of demoness and destroyer.

Proctor parallels the figures of Caliban and Ariel, combining in one body and mind both the rude, gross savage and the ethereal spirit.

Proctor is by turns brutal and menacing and gentle and innocent; he is dim-witted and ignorant and he is cunning, resourceful, and perceptive; at once a drunken sot and a delicate acrobat. It is Proctor with whom Maitland has the deepest psychic affinity, the two sharing clothes, a wristwatch, a name, and ultimately a tomb. Although ostensibly it is Maitland who masters Proctor, it is the latter who exerts the real power: introducing Maitland to a "new time setting" (86), awakening him to the life of the unconscious. Upon Proctor's death, Maitland assumes the tramp-acrobat's ability to read the grass by touch, and may also be said to have inherited the island from him. Proctor personifies the deepest instincts and impulses of the psyche: anger and love, the urge for oblivion and the urge for transcendence, all the aspects of the unconscious self that Maitland has neglected and suppressed in the past. In the course of his sojourn on the island he learns to recognize and appreciate and finally to integrate them into his life and identity.

Concrete Island affirms again the primacy, persistence, and power of the unconscious, whose unseen energies withstand the hegemony of the ego-mind. The forces of the unconscious, the author tells us, will abide and prevail:

> he inspected the island more carefully. Comparing it with the motorway system, he saw that it was far older than the surrounding terrain, as if this triangular patch of waste ground had survived by the exercise of a unique guile and persistence, and would continue to survive, unknown and disregarded, long after the motorways had collapsed into dust. (50)

In a similar manner, though with a somewhat different emphasis, Ballard's next novel, *High Rise*,[5] also affirms the powers of the unconscious, demonstrating in this instance the futility and the peril of attempting to deny or restrain its energies. The embodiment of such suppression of the unconscious in the novel is the high-rise of the title, a newly built, forty-story apartment building of glass and concrete, "a small vertical city" (9) inhabited by a population of two thousand well-to-do urban professionals. Shortly after full occupancy of the building is achieved, the residents undergo a collective psychosis, resulting in appalling violence and in the breakdown of all civilized values.

Although no direct allusion is made in *High Rise* to the biblical story of the tower of Babel, the two tales possess certain affinities. In both instances the construction is undertaken, we may say, in a spirit of hubris. The high-rise, we are told, "seemed almost to challenge the sun itself," and would at first seem to have been successful in its attempt to "colonize the sky" (19). In the case both of the tower of Babel and of the high-rise, retribution is visited upon them by what we may term the fundamental, unseen powers of the world. And both enterprises conclude in a confoundment of language. Whether deliberate on the author's part or fortuitous, the parallels between the stories are significant, suggesting both the presumptuous ignorance and overweening vanity of humankind and the might of the forces against which we offend.

The catalyst of the psychic devolution of the residents of the high-rise is the building itself, whose "arid and affectless" (36) environment promotes the anonymity and the isolation of its inhabitants, even while its "glut of conveniences" (9), its luxury, privacy, and efficiency pander to the weakest and most frivolous aspects of their characters. Outwardly successful, satisfied and optimistic specimens of a new affluent social type, "the first to master a new kind of twentieth-century life" (36), the residents of the high-rise are inwardly destitute and desperate, consumed with loathing for themselves, for each other, and for the building. So utterly, unbearably "eventless" are their lives when considered in any terms other than those of self-gratification that the reckless, convulsive response of their unconscious in the face of such "decerebration" (36) is to embrace atavism, to destroy the symbol and instrument of their psychic oppression: the high-rise.

The high-rise is repeatedly likened to a zoo, and indeed, we are told that "Zoos and the architecture of large structures" had always been the "particular interest" (80) of the architect of the high-rise, Anthony Royal. At one point, after the outbreak of violence in the building, Royal admits that "Without knowing it, he had constructed a gigantic vertical zoo, its hundreds of cages stacked above each other" (134). Another recurrent simile for the high-rise is that of a prison. One character, Richard Wilder, is reminded by his apartment "of a cell . . . in the psychiatric wing of the prison" (44). Another resident of the high-rise, Dr. Robert Laing, compares his flat to a "cell" (7), and likens his leaving the building in order to go to work to the release of a convict "after a long prison-sentence" (101). Even the architect himself acknowledges the high-rise as constituting a "fur-lined prison" (81).

This depiction of the high-rise as a zoo and a prison is further supported and extended by a cluster of images of constriction and oppression. Despite the ample space and even in some cases the magnitude of their flats, the residents of the high-rise nevertheless regard themselves as being "boxed up" (9, 81), and many of them also feel weighed down by the vast dimensions of the building. The insomnia so widespread among the residents would seem to be a symptom of their collective sense of psychic compression. Wilder develops "a powerful phobia about the high-rise," becoming "constantly aware of the immense weight of concrete stacked above him" and feeling suffocated by the sensation of "each of the 999 other apartments pressing on him through the walls and ceiling, forcing the air from his chest" (48). Other residents, too, are oppressed by "the image of the building in their own minds, the multiplying layers of concrete that anchored them to the floor" (58). Royal, as well, on a visit down into the building from his aerial penthouse on the topmost floor of the high-rise, feels himself "crushed by the pressure of all the people above him, by the thousands of individual lives, each with its pent-up time and space" (88).

The reaction of the residents of the high-rise to their sense of an intolerable confinement and compression of their lives and identities takes the form of a sudden, violent revolt against all order and rationality and a release of all their repressed hostilities and aggressions. Fractionalized according to the floors on which they live, the inhabitants of the high-rise engage in destruction of the services of the building and in violent confrontations among factions or "clans" that quickly escalate into full-scale warfare. In the course of only a few months the residents revert from enlightened, civilized human beings through stages of feudalism and tribalism to barbarism and utter savagery.

The atavistic descent of the residents of the high-rise is accompanied by a corresponding decline in language ability from a fully intelligible, articulate level of expression to pre-verbal grunts, clicks, and cries. At the same time, they separate themselves entirely from the outside world, no longer going to their jobs, severing all means of communication with the world outside the high-rise, and, at last, isolating themselves inside their separate apartments. In a metaphoric sense, their abandonment of language and their separation from external reality may be seen as a parallel to the catatonic withdrawal of a terminal psychotic. Like the Pyros of "The Concentration City" or the subjects of the narcotomy experiment in "Manhole 69," the residents of the high-rise are victims of rationality and technology, whose only means of resistance to the unbearable psychic tensions generated by the suppression of the unconscious is compulsive destruction and madness. In this regard, *High Rise* also prefigures one of the author's most recent works, *Running Wild*.

The central motif of *High Rise* consists of recurrent imagery of darkness and obscurity, suggesting the encroaching mental and moral darkness of the inhabitants of the building, and the increasing narrowing of their awareness and the diminution of their consciousness. At the outset of the novel, there are electrical failures of only a few minutes' duration that cause darkness in the building. These are followed by permanent black-outs that leave entire floors without lights, making "dark bands" which at night "stretch across the face of the high-rise like dead strata in a fading brain" (75). The number of floors in complete darkness increases steadily until by the end of the novel all the floors of the high-rise are in darkness, as are also the minds and spirits of its inhabitants.

In a similar manner, the vision of the residents is gradually obscured from without and within. Following the fateful drowning of the Afghan dog, there is an "almost palpable miasma" (22) in the area of the swimming pool. Later a similar mist, "a faint interior luminosity" (145), is to be found throughout the building, illuminating it with "a dim light, pearled by a faint interior glow . . . a miasma secreted by the high-rise itself, distillation of all its dead concrete" (150). At the same time, Laing remarks how his sight, "dulled by being used chiefly at night, presented him with an increasingly opaque world" (146), and Wilder also finds his visual perception "screened . . . by a faint mist" (164). This motif of darkness and obscurity is even more striking and effective when considered in contrast to Ballard's customary use of light imagery to suggest the proximity or presence of an ontological Eden. The high-rise, its elevation notwithstanding, clearly represents a nether world, a realm of lost and damned souls.

High Rise is cautionary in character, depicting the law of action and reaction as applied to the energies of the human psyche. Like a powerful spring that is compressed more and more tightly into a smaller and smaller mass until it escapes or is released from the pressure that contracts it, the reaction of the unconscious to the suppressive force exerted upon it by the conscious mind will be equal in strength and opposite in direction. Overcoming the constraining agency that has held it in check, it will recoil with intense and furious force. As the novel demonstrates, the sudden liberation of such psychic energies after long restraint may be devastating in effect.

High Rise concludes what may be regarded as a quartet of interrelated books treating the theme of contemporary urban-technological life, its perilous psychic imbalance, and its latent redemptive energies which express themselves through disaster. In these four books Ballard views our age as one fraught with unique dangers and opportunities. The author warns us against succumbing to the pressures brought to bear upon us by our rational-technological environment and becoming "like an advanced species of machine" (35), and against the hazards inherent in a surrender to atavism as a desperate reaction to the sterility and dehumanization of our lives. And he affirms once again a fundamental faith in the powers of the unconscious by whose mysterious office we may discover—in the unlikely and the unwonted, in the wayward and the perverse, even in the very products of technology—means of attaining liberation and of repossessing authentic being.

4

"Trapped Aircraft": The Later Short Fiction

A dominant theme in Ballard's short fiction of the period 1966 to 1989 is that of illusion: the misapprehensions we are content to accept and the self-deceptions we practice with regard to the nature of reality and of our own identity, and the deliberate limitations and restrictions imposed upon our awareness and our consciousness from without for purposes of manipulation and control. The dangerous and even fatal consequences of illusion, and the ways we can attain release from the constraints and restraints of illusion are central concerns of the author throughout these later stories.

In the story "Tomorrow is a Million Years"[1] Ballard depicts the treacherous and tenacious nature of illusion through the character of Glanville, a fugitive from justice who, together with his wfie, has sought sanctuary on a remote, uninhabited planet. The reader perceives the events of the story from Glanville's point of view, accepting his motivations and interpretations at face value until the very end of the tale when it becomes apparent that Glanville is completely mad. Glanville is, in fact, a psychotic killer who has murdered and mutilated his wife, though in his deluded state he persists in believing her to be alive, seeing her clearly before him and conversing with her.

Glanville embodies the very type of the self-deceiving person, who, rejecting for selfish reasons the claims of the invisible world and divorcing himself utterly from his true identity, must inevitably become the victim and prisoner of his own illusions. As Thornwald, the police officer who has pursued Glanville to his place of hiding observes, "You've built your own little world here"; noting, though, that it is a "gilded hell" (38), an hallucinated prison that is far more confining and more terrible than any in which Glanville could be incarcerated for his crimes. Abandoned in the end by Thornwald to endure his own self-inflicted torments, Glanville's situation—alone, in exile on a distant, desert planet, afflicted by terrors of his own creation—serves to emblematize the ultimate condition of illusion, the inferno of absolute ego-mind.

An allusion to Coleridge's "The Rime of the Ancient Mariner" casts Glanville in the role of the Mariner whose punishment for his heedless, selfish act of violence is undertaken by the female spirit known as "the Nightmare Life-in-Death." Like that of the Mariner, Glanville's crime may be seen to represent a denial of the primary reality of the unseen world and a transgression against his own deepest nature, though unlike the Mariner's there is no indication given here that Glanville's sufferings will refine him or lead him to greater moral and metaphysical awareness. The character of the retribution visited upon both the Mariner and Glanville is the same, however, a living death.

The "Ancient Mariner" parallel and the desert imagery of "Tomorrow is a Million Years" also figure prominently in "Cry Hope, Cry Fury,"[2] another story centered upon the theme of illusion. In this instance the Mariner figure, Robert Melville, succeeds in expiating his guilt through love, while it is the witch figure of Nightmare Life-in-Death, Hope Cunard, who remains trapped in a living death of illusion.

Hope is the prisoner of her own illusions in the form of her obsessive, unrequited love for Charles Rademaeker and in the shape of the mythic and literary patterns that she projects upon experience. Moreover, she is also the victim of elaborately staged effects produced by her half-brother, Foyle, and his lover, in order to deceive and to control her. After making a desperate, futile, final "attempt to break through the illusions multiplying around her and reach some kind of reality" (108–9), she surrenders to the gaudy, empty stage-world manipulated by Foyle, yielding completely to the arid, desert realm of illusion. Her ultimate fate is similar to that of Glanville in the preceeding story, for as her former lover, Rademaeker, pronounces: "She's alone now . . . forever" (108).

That the consequences of illusion can also be deadly in a literal sense as well as a figurative sense is illustrated by the story "The Dead Astronaut,"[3] in which a man and his wife, Philip and Judith Groves, lose their lives as the result of their delusional obsessions. Judith refuses to accept the death of her former lover, the astronaut Robert Hamilton who was killed in an accident in space twenty years previously; she is preoccupied with his memory and with the notion of his eventual return to earth from his orbiting space capsule. Her husband, acting out of his own obsessions, arranges to purchase Hamilton's mortal remains from relic hunters when the astronaut's space capsule finally leaves its orbit and crashes on earth. However, far from achieving fulfillment, satisfaction, or surcease from sorrow, the Groves are fatally poisoned by Hamilton's radioactive ashes, which prove to have been contaminated by a nuclear weapon carried on board his space capsule. The story suggests that illusion and obsession are forms of psychic poison, undermining our lives and our minds, first weakening and ruining them by degrees, and finally destroying them.

The destruction of human life as a result of illusion occurs also in "Say Goodbye to the Wind."[4] In this story the chief symbol of illusion is the clothing made of bio-fabric, which has become fashionable to the exclusion (except among the unchic) of all "inert" fabrics. The counter symbol to the vanity and empty ostentation represented by the bio-fabric fashions is nakedness. "Naked we came into this world, naked we leave it" (130) quotes the narrator, Mr. Samson, owner of a bio-fabric fashion boutique, while one of his elegant, celebrity customers, Raine Channing, confides her secret dislike of bio-fabrics: "Do you know, though, a few months ago I hated them? I really wanted everyone in the world to go naked, so that all the clothes would die" (133). At the end of the story Samson is left naked, after he is rescued from a suit of bio-fabric which attempted to kill him.

The near-suffocation of the narrator by a bio-fabric garment may be seen as symbolic of the asphyxiation of our true identity and our human potential by illusion. Indeed, we learn that the previous owner of the suit, a bio-fabric designer, was strangled by his own clothes. Significantly, too, Samson's rescuer is dressed in so-called "inert" clothes, a beachcomber, a natural man.

The other symbol of illusion in the story is cosmetic surgery undertaken for reasons of glamour and vanity. The resultant facial "mask" (132, 143) perpetrates an illusion of youth and beauty upon the beholder while it imprisons the "occupant" of the mask in a world of falsehood and self-deception. Raine Channing, who has undergone numerous such operations in order to retain an apperance of teenage-ingenue beauty, ultimately forfeits her real identity to the mask. As a result, her life-drive and creative impulses are perverted, assuming the form of destructive urges. Only at night, when she dreams and sleepwalks, does she briefly recover her own identity, which survives only at an unconscious level. In this regard, she becomes an emblem of all modern, alienated humanity, undone by vanity and illusion.

Other Ballard stories of this period describe the varieties of illusion, the myriad phantoms, shadows, hallucinations, and mirages that we pursue or flee from, live and die for. "The Beach Murders"[5] is a case in point, a story of intrigue, ruthlessness, betrayal, violence, and death, all of which occur, ostensibly, in the furtherance of ideological ends. The endless intricacies and complications of the plot serve ultimately to communicate a sense of the fundamental meaninglessness of the events, their lack of coherence or real purpose. What we finally perceive in this tangled web of international espionage (which both sides would doubtless claim is undertaken to advance the cause of human liberation) is people living according to confusions, and killing and dying for illusions.

The deflection and consequent waste of our energies and our attention by obsession and illusion is the subject of a parable-like story titled "The Smile."[6] The narrator of the story, a middle-aged bachelor, purchases what he believes to be a life-size manikin of a woman in an antique shop, only to discover that it is "no manikin but a once-living woman, her peerless skin mounted and preserved by a master, not of the dollmaker's, but of the taxidermist's art" (170). The infatuation of the narrator with this inert object (which bears the name Serena Cockayne), this mere husk of life, the care and devotion he bestows upon it, the agonies of jealousy he suffers on its behalf, may be seen as a correlative of our own misdirected admiration for and cultivation of illusions.

Like the figures in other Ballard stories who strive after phantoms or false idols, the narrator of "The Smile" soon becomes a prisoner of his obsession. Ultimately he derives no pleasure or satisfaction from it; instead it is the occasion of unceasing self-reproach and torment. At the conclusion of the story, he waits passively for an end to his imprisonment: "I am completely bound to Serena . . . Helplessly watching her smile . . . I wait for her to die and set me free" (177). Even should Serena "die" somehow, we may question whether the narrator will ever succeed in liberating himself from illusion, so wholly has he given himself over to its compelling influence and attraction. Like Glanville, Raine Channing or Hope Cunard in the preceding stories, the narrator of "The Smile" embodies that ruinous weakness of the human psyche: to embrace and, in turn, to be embraced by illusion.

That our predisposition to accept a comfortable illusion in lieu of an unpleasant truth makes us ready victims of forces that seek to practice deception upon us for purposes of their own profit and advantage is the theme of "Having a Wonderful Time."[7] The story depicts the seduction of large numbers of people drawn from the modern European work force, both blue-collar and white-collar workers and even persons holding managerial positions, by irresistibly cheap vacations to sunny Mediterranean holiday resorts where they are then kept permanently. Their captivity is so gradual, so subtle, and so agreeable that they are not even aware of it, while its purpose is to draw away redundant and unemployable people from their native countries, where they might eventually constitute a destabilizing or even a potentially revolutionary factor.

One such holiday prisoner attempts to alarm the others and to form a resistance group but he fails to arouse any response among his fellow captives, who are too busy swimming, water-skiing, drinking, and sunning themselves. The only ones to take him seriously are the authorities, who eliminate him quietly and unobtrusively by arranging a boating accident. The story raises unsettling questions concerning how much we may already find ourselves in such a fur-lined prison, how much we are being pacified by the myriad distractions and comforts we enjoy, and how much we may have forfeited our freedom and authentic being for the pleasures of a society that is already a "permanent holiday camp" (48).

The motif of a manipulated, illusory reality created for the purpose of allaying fear, anger, and disquiet among the populace is also treated in "The Secret History of World War III."[8] In this instance a collusion between the government and the media of the United States exists to distract the citizen-viewer-readers from the grave crises and ominous events of the period by smothering such items of news under floods of trivia and by creating pseudo-events to engage national attention. Perilous developments abroad and major foreign policy decisions made by the President and his advisors in response to these increasingly critical situations are relegated to the back pages of newspapers and limited to quick phrases on the radio and television news. In this manner, World War III—a brief, non-fatal nuclear exchange between the United States and the USSR—passes unremarked and goes unremembered.

Ballard suggests that this sort of manipulation, this manufacturing of reality, would be impossible were it not for our innate desire to ignore what is disturbing and disagreeable to us. In a sense the real collusion may be seen to be between ourselves and the media: we prefer, indeed we insist upon, a world of illusion. At the same time, precisely because we refuse to acknowledge the dangers that exist around us, these dangers multiply and intensify. Ultimately, as other Ballard stories dealing with this theme have warned us, indulgence in illusion is inevitably fatal.

The story "War Fever"[9] represents a further elaboration upon the theme of illusion, presenting another situation in which a fabricated, fraudulent reality is deliberately imposed upon a group of people for purposes of manipulation and control. Set about thirty years in the future, "War Fever" depicts the strife-torn city of Beirut, with its numerous warring factions and their continually shifting alliances, being used as a psychological laboratory by the United Nations. Unknown to the participants in the endless civil war—who are orphaned children from all over the globe—the entire conflict has been instigated and is being perpetuated by the U.N., as an experimental study in what that organization regards as the psychological virus of the martial spirit. The combatants are in reality no more than "rats in the war lab" (110), fighting and dying for falsehoods that have been foisted upon them.

Although the story seems pessimistic in tone with regard to the human capacity for cruelty and violence, for treachery and for gullibility, it also affirms the abiding desire of humankind for peace, as evidenced by the temporary cease-fire agreement achieved through the inspiration and efforts of one person. And although the short-lived peace is sabotaged by U.N. observers, it nonetheless remains a poignant and powerful sign of our deepest and most heartfelt hopes for the world. Moreover, Ballard suggests that the hatred which fuels the conflict is a perversion of the primary emotion of love—as witness the love of the main character, Ryan, for Valentina and for his sister and his aunt—a perversion rendered possible only through ignorance and fear and by the deliberate distortion of the truth undertaken by the U.N. with their relentless propaganda campaign—newsreels of enemy atrocities and the ubiquitous atrocity-photograph posters plastered on walls throughout the city—all serving to establish and maintain a "propaganda stranglehold" (100) on the mind.

"War Fever" also affirms the spontaneous and irresistible power latent in the psyche to resist deception and manipulation through the faculty of vision, by which I mean that mode of perception by which essences are discerned behind appearances and a transcendental whole is glimpsed behind the various disparate parts. An instance of such visionary awareness occurs at the beginning of the story when, during a fire-fight in a ruined hotel, Ryan perceives "a fleeting halo" (92) of sunlight and dust illuminating the derelict replica of a tropical island that stands in the atrium, the relic of a cheerful and elegant past, transforming it for a few seconds into a vision of a lost paradise. It is precisely at this moment that Ryan conceives his idea of a cease-fire that might secure a permanent peace, a vision that quickly gathers urgency as a consequence of the death of the "cherubic" (94) and portentously named Angel Porrua in the rubble-filled miniature lagoon of the island. Although this vision is ultimately betrayed, it is not invalidated. Despite repeated deferments and failures it will persist until it prevails.

Technology, in these stories, is viewed as an extension of pseudo-consciousness and an ally of illusion, serving to alienate humankind from authentic identity and to perpetuate a sort of chic and flashy life-in-death. In "The Impossible Man,"[10] for example, the advances of medical science, including organ transplants and restorative surgery, have reached a point where human life can be prolonged "more or less indefinitely" (183). After an initial period of enthusiasm for the new immortality, however, interest in it drops sharply as more and more people chose not to extend their lives beyond their natural span, recognizing that such a life lacks meaning and authenticity.

Conrad Foster, the protagonist of the story, is one of the rare young people in a world of the aged. Conrad loses his leg in a traffic accident and receives a transplanted limb in its place. But although the new limb is sound and strong, he cannot accept it emotionally and feels that "its presence seemed to diminish him, in someway subtracting rather than adding to his own sense of identity" (190). In the end, Conrad choses to reject the leg and to divest himself of it in order to preserve his personal integrity. The responses of both Conrad and of the aged to the achievements of medical technology serve to indicate an essential incompatibility between the aims and values of science and those of the human spirit.

Similarly, in "The 60 Minute Zoom"[11] technology is shown to be a force that caters to and exploits the weaknesses of ego-mind, nourishing our basest motives and appetites while at the same time hindering and arresting the processes of individuation and of self-realization. The narrator of the story is a sort of camera-voyeur whose erotic fixation is upon the private behavior of his neighbors and of his wife, upon whom he spies through the medium of the zoom lens of his camera. The narrative concerns his attempt to make the "ultimate home movie" (134)—the most recent of many such that he has filmed—recording his wife's infidelity, shot from a distance of 300 yards.

The narrator is unable to confront life unmediated by the camera lens, in the same way that he is unable to relate to others, including his wife, except insofar as they embody means to his own selfish gratification. With regard to his wife, he acknowledges: "I prefer her seen through a lens . . . emblematic of my own needs and fantasies rather than existing in her own right" (138). The camera lens provides a "reductive authority" (139) the narrator finds agreeable, an angle of vision that renders the world and sexuality in particular unthreateningly abstract. But its diminished, distorted perspectives constitute a form of blindness, both perceptual and moral. It is this dehumanizing blindness to which the narrator's wife, Helen, alludes when as an act of provocation she symbolically blinds her husband's cherished inflatable plastic seahorse, itself an emblem of his arested development, as well as an analogue of his empty, inauthentic identity.

So deep and so complete is the state of absorption induced in the narrator by the long-distance viewfinder of his camera that in the end not only does he slay his wife in revenge for spoiling his "ultimate home movie" but he also simultaneously beholds himself doing so through the zoom lens of his camera. The man has at last become an appendage of the camera, his human identity assimilated by the instrument of his obsession.

As I read the story, the camera may be seen as a metaphor for technology which, under the guise of extending and enlarging our perception, systematically diminishes our awareness and restricts our consciousness. Like the nameless narrator of the story, we allow technology to distract us from the real business of our lives; we surrender to the false sense of power which it provides, and thus ultimately are led to deny and to destroy that aspect of ourselves with which we most urgently require communication and reconciliation.

The ruthless, expansionist character of the technological mentality, its drive to subdue and to root out other modes of consciousness, provides the theme for two closely related stories: "The Killing Ground"[12] and "Theatre of War."[13] In both stories the United States of America serves as the embodiment of the scientific-technological mentality, while the United Kingdom (or its insurgent National Liberation Army) represents natural consciousness expressed in an agrarian, communal culture based upon alternative technology.

In the first story, rebel bands of Britons, ragged, under-fed, ill-equipped, and poorly armed, resist the invading military forces of the United States, whose soldiers are armed with an array of the most modern weaponry, supported by air, and "protected by an immense technology of warfare" (115). Indeed, as we are told: "American weapons technology had advanced to the point where it made almost no sense at all to the rebel commanders. Artillery fire, battle dispositions and helicopter raids were now computer-directed, patrols and sorties programmed ahead. The American equipment was so sophisticated that even the wrist-watches stripped off dead prisoners were too complicated to read" (117).

The superiority of their armaments notwithstanding, the Americans are slowly losing the war in the U.K., which is, in fact, only one action in what has become "a world Viet Nam" (115), a global struggle between technology and the new agrarian order, a sort of post-industrial culture. The ultimate outcome of the conflict seems hopeful for the forces of the latter which, in contrast to the former, also possess a cultural dynamism and an evolutionary potential:

> the war had turned the entire population of Europe into an armed peasantry, the first intelligent agrarian community since the eighteenth century. *That* peasantry had produced the Industrial Revolution. This one, literally burrowing like some advanced species of termite into the sub-soil of the twentieth century, might in time produce something greater. (118)

A recurrent image in the story is that of oil-stained water, suggesting not only the pollution of the natural world by technology, but also the nature of the story's two adversary forces: water, life-giving, protean, capable of endurance and of self-generation; and oil, a life-denying, defiling agent, whose contaminating presence upon the water is in reality shallow and superficial, limited to the surface. In the course of natural processes, oil will dissipate and ultimately disappear. In this sense, the hegemony of the rational-scientific-technological mind may be seen as a vain endeavor, a finally transitory phenomenon in the evolution of human consciousness.

Whereas technology serves to abet illusion and pseudo-consciousness, these conditions are resisted and subverted by forces of the unconscious and the superconscious. In a series of stories from this period the author affirms again the potency of these energies latent in the human psyche, as well as those originating from a non-human or sur-human dimension of reality, in opposing the various agencies of ego-mind and illusion.

In "The Greatest Television Show on Earth"[14] the human appetite for pleasure in the form of violent and exotic entertainment is rebuked by a primal force more powerful than all of technology. The story concerns the commercial exploitation of the discovery of time travel at the hands of television corporations who transmit the major events of the past to their jaded twenty-first-century viewers. The selection of the events to be broadcast is governed by their intrinsic entertainment value, with the "emphasis on death and destruction" (149). Certain historical events are even "re-scripted" by the networks, that is, they are enhanced and heightened in the tradition of Cecil B. De Mille, in order to achieve more spectacular effects for the titillation of the Time Vision audience.

This hubris and unholy historical voyeurism is brought to a summary end, however, when the networks attempt to transmit the flight of the Israelites from Egypt and the crossing of the Red Sea. This meticulously orchestrated and lavishly embellished spectacle is suddenly interrupted in mid-transmission. After an interval of two hours, transmission resumes but only for a brief instant, just long enough to reveal the wreckage of all the television and time-travel equipment and the loss of the camera crews in the swirling waters of the Red Sea. Aside from the shocking loss of life and materiel, and the striking fact that the last, brief transmission is sent *after* the destruction of all the Time Vision equipment, what most astonishes the viewers with regard to the second and final transmission is "the eerie light that illuminated the picture, as if some archaic but extraordinary method of power were being used to transmit it (154).

In this manner are the trivial and superficial desires of the ego-mind checked, and human presumption reproved by the power of the superconscious. On a very small scale, a similar principle to that informing Ballard's tales of cataclysm and disaster may be seen to be operative here. There are boundaries, we are cautioned, beyond which our frenzied appetites for pleasure must not transgress. To do so invites calamity. The story also serves to remind us that whatever the extent of our powers—our material, technological powers—there are powers unfathomably greater than ours. It would behoove us, therefore, to learn to think and to act accordingly.

The relationship of ordinary human consciousness to the superconscious is further examined in "The Life and Death of God."[15] The story is a reversal of the old dictum that if there were no God it would be necessary to create Him, which here becomes: if we were certain that there were a God it would be necessary to deny His existence.

In the story the announcement of conclusive scientific proof of the existence of a supreme being causes a sweeping transformation of human society: neurosis and vice disappear, police forces are disbanded, armies demobilized, and a universal euphoria and sense of millennial expectation prevail among the peoples of the earth. Before long, however, there is a general slackening, followed by a slump, of commerce, industry and agriculture as people lose interest in such mundane pursuits; the new sense of morality renders numerous jobs obsolete. As the world economy breaks down and services collapse, the old survival instinct, pleasure principle, and sense of the practical re-assert themselves, and, ultimately, to the immense relief of everyone, the theologians announce that "God is Dead" (147).

The poles of the story are, at one extreme, the concept of an "intelligent being of infinite dimension" (139) whose existence pervades the universe; and at the other extreme, the commercial, selfish, hypocritical celebration of Christmas amid mounting world tensions, the image with which the story concludes. The interior movement of the story is from the first pole to the last, depicting in this fashion the tenacity and resilience of the ego-mind with its endless ingenuity for ignoring or disputing or disavowing all that is inimical to self-gratification. The story points up the way in which we resist information subversive to our identities, cherishing our habits and appetites in preference to illumination or enlargement of a spiritual character.

The futility of all the shifts and dodges that we undertake to maintain our discrete ego-identities, our self-conscious selfhoods, is illustrated in two closely related tales: "The Intensive Care Unit"[16] and "Motel Architecture."[17] The first story takes place in a future society in which each human being lives alone and in strict isolation from all human contact except via telescreen. In fact, ordinances exist to prevent physical contact in any form, and even "to meet another human being [is] an indictable offense" (197). Despite such prohibitions and despite the "complex of security precautions . . . the electronic alarm signals, steel grilles, and gastight doors" (202) that heremetically seal each individual from all contact with the world outside, one man contrives to meet the members of his family, his wife and children, bringing them together for a family reunion, as it were, in his dwelling.

That the family reunion erupts into violence and mutual hatred seems less to confirm the wisdom of collective isolation than to indicate that such a sterile, barren life as their society requires and enforces creates unconscious retributory energies, forces uncontrollable by the conscious mind. When at last these long-accumulated and strictly repressed energies are given expression they are explosively violent and destructive. The story suggests once again that thwarted tenderness, blocked or frustrated love becomes a sort of black hole in the psyche, a field of negative energy which expresses itself as hatred and violence.

The second story postulates a similar future society in which the majority of people live in willing isolation from others inside structures called solaria. Their only contact with other human beings is limited to the visits made periodically by the personnel who maintain the services of the solaria, repairmen noted for their unobtrusive, silent efficiency. The main character of "Motel Architecture," a man named Pangborn, suspects that there is an intruder hiding in his solarium. In the beginning Pangborn can only hear the breathing of the stranger, smell his body odors, but soon more tangible evidences come to light: a footprint, used towels, the remains of hasty meals taken in secret, fleeting glimpses on the internal camera monitor of a moving figure. After two attempts upon his life by the intruder—the first with sleeping tablets in his coffee, the second with a knife—Pangborn ultimately discovers that the intruder is himself. Wishing definitively to escape from the sounds and smells of his own body, and from the presence of a hostile alien consciousness resident within himself, Pangborn takes his own life.

"Motel Architecture" is a parable of self-estrangement, of the attempt by the ego-mind to create an artificial, insular, inward world of complete self-sufficiency, and of the power of the unconscious to disturb and to destroy such a world. Pangborn's surmise at one point in the story that the intruder is "an exhausted fugitive from some act of mis-justice, a wrongly incarcerated mental patient" (187), proves to be true on a symbolic level, for the hostile intruder is his own unknown, repressed self, the aspects of his life and identity that he has wrongfully persecuted, exiled, and imprisoned. For even within the isolated world of the solarium Pangborn has, by his narrow, inflexible tastes and habits, created "a small second world within the private universe of the solarium" (183), a prison within a prison. Moreover, as he acknowledges: "Fantasy and imagination had always played little part in his life, and he felt only at home within the framework of an absolute realism" (184).

This cherished "realism," however, proves to be an artificial, atrophied life of ennui and secret despair, a life-in-death whose only spark of interest or excitement derives from Pangborn's morbid obsession with the film *Psycho*, in particular with the famous shower scene. Pangborn's fixation upon this film and this particular scene is emblematic of his psychic condition, for like the character of the schizophrenic murderer in the movie, Pangborn is a deeply, irreconcilably divided man whose conscious and unconscious selves are locked in a deadly conflict. And like the killer in *Psycho*, Pangborn murders a woman who embodies the vitality and life-force that he most needs yet most fears and loathes. The consequence of this act is his own death. The murder of the woman maintenance worker metaphorically prefigures it, for in killing the life-affirming, invigorating figure of the woman Pangborn has definitively denied the life of the unconscious, of the imagination, the life of the body and the affections, in favor of the arid and sterile life of the mind. As in other tales by Ballard, the resistance or denial of the imperatives of the unconscious inevitably results in disastrous retribution being visited upon the isolate intellect, the fortress ego.

As the title "A Host of Furious Fancies"[18] suggests, the imagination or the unconscious assumes anew a vengeful role in this story as well, and once again it does so in reaction to the repressive actions of the rational intelligence, the ego-mind. The narrator of the story, Dr. Charcot, is another deeply divided man. Like certain other of Ballard's characters, such as the narrator of "The 60 Minute Zoom" or Pangborn in "Motel Architecture," he is in a state of psychic disconnection or discord so radical that aspects of his consciousness have become completely separated from each other, existing as autonomous entities. He observes his own behavior as if it were that of another person, but is unable to alter it.

The cause of this condition lies in Dr. Charcot's earlier scrupulously rational, scientific orientation. He was raised according to the tenets of skepticism and empiricism and he fully embraced the principles of this tradition as an adult. As an established medical doctor with a comfortable practice, Charcot remains dubious of all that is not physical or material, especially conditions of the psyche: "Since my earliest days as a medical student I had been hostile to all the claims made by psychotherapy, the happy hunting ground of pseudo-scientific cranks of an especially dangerous kind" (55). Appropriately, he is a dermatologist, unable or unwilling to see more than skin-deep as it were, incapable of perceiving realities behind appearances. The punishment of Dr. Charcot's presumption in first denying and then meddling with the invisible powers of the psyche is to assume irrevocably the delusion of one of his patients. As the story's imagery of incarceration suggests, Dr. Charcot is self-condemned to inhabit "a special kind of prison" (51).

The larger prison, the prison in which we are all incarcerated and of which Dr. Charcot's personal prison is but a cell, is the prison compounded of fraud, falsehood, and illusion, of space and time and matter, the vast, fast prison of the phenomenological universe. Our unconscious urge to demolish this prison and to repossess true being manifests itself, as we have seen throughout Ballard's fiction, in various manners and guises, most often of a wayward, aberrant, or unpredictable character. In "The Object of the Attack"[19] this desire for deliverance expresses itself through the mind and will of a psychotic, epileptic mystic and would-be assassin named Matthew Young.

Young is a strange and compelling figure, a curious compound of a sort of purity and simplicity and of cunning and resourcefulness, of devotional fervor and of murderous violence. Imprisoned for an assassination attempt upon Her Majesty the Queen and the President of the United States, Young eventually escapes by means of an illusion, the construction of an Ames room to confound camera surveillance. His real target, however, is the American ex-astronaut, Colonel Thomas Jefferson Stamford, a dangerously ambitious megalomaniac and self-proclaimed "Space-Age Messiah" (7) whose international popularity is rising and whose influence upon world affairs is growing apace.

Stamford and Young are counterparts, each embodying qualities exactly antithetical to the other. The former, though ostensibly religious, is, in fact, "as demented as Hitler" (10), planning a kind of nuclear crusade, a holy war, against the Soviet Union and the non-Christian world. Stamford with his various publicity gimmicks, his shrewd manipulation of the media, and his showbiz tricks and effects, employs illusion in the service of illusion. Young, while seemingly violent and mentally disturbed, is, in fact, devoutly spiritual and by any standards saner than Stamford, whom Young regards as "a false Messiah" (8). Young, too, uses illusion (principally the Ames room) in the furtherance of his mission, but he does so in order to dismantle illusion and to free himself and humankind from the prison of "the continuum of time and space" (6).

Both men are, in each his way, associated with light, but with two distinctly different qualities of light. Whereas Stamford's characteristic illumination is "trick lighting" and that of "a light show with laser graphics" (8), and he is also an advocate of laser weaponry, Young suffers from a form of "hysterical photophobia" (4), exhibiting a painful reaction to the harsh artificial lighting of the prison punishment cell, while at the same time he is profoundly moved by the artistic depiction of "serene light over the visionary meadows" (4) and "the light of a true nature" (9). Likewise, both men are associated with flight, again in ways that are diametrically opposed to each other. Stamford is associated with the military-technological extensions of flight, with the exploitation of outer space; whereas Young is identified with the aeronautics of man-powered or wind-powered aircraft, that is to say pure flight, and with the exploration of inner space.

Stamford may thus be seen to embody the aspirations of the ego-mind to control the temporal-material universe, while Young accordingly may be seen to embody the deep-seated urges of the psyche to transcend time and space and the limitations of personal consciousness. The story represents a further testimony to the capacity of the unconscious to withstand the forces and effects of the physical, time-space universe, and to persist in attempting to effect our common rescue from that condition of being.

Although a figure such as Matthew Young may be infused and imbued with the power of the unconscious to the degree that he becomes virtually an incarnation or an instrument of that energy, such power is latent in each human psyche, awaiting only arousal and opportunity of expression. The universality of the appetite for transcendence and of the desire to attain true identity and being are manifestations of this power, while certain inexplicable drives and compulsions or irresistible fascinations to which we may be subject represent summons from the realm of the unconscious, calls to embark upon a quest for identity and transcendence. In common with the author's earlier fiction, a number of Ballard's stories from this period are concerned with this quest and with the inner process of recognition and submission that is a necessary accompaniment of the quest.

In "The Day of Forever"[20] the summons from the unconscious takes the form of a dream whose haunting elusiveness and recurrence at last compel the dreamer, a man named Halliday, to undertake a journey in search of the actual scene and the real-life counterpart of the figure in his vision. Halliday's quest takes place against the background of an earth which is no longer rotating. It is divided into zones of static time. In search of the realization of his dream, whose central image is that of a "woman who walked through colonnades in a world without shadows" (8), Halliday travels from the endless day of northern Europe to the perpetual dusk of North Africa.

There, he encounters a woman named Gabrielle Szabo who corresponds to the figure from his dream, together with her sinister companion, Dr. Mallory. Halliday follows them south and east into the desert, across the slowly advancing line of darkness. For a period he resists the timelessness and the darkness of the desert and his fascination with Gabrielle, secretly maintaining a temporal orientation by means of a wristwatch and a collection of clocks. Finally, renouncing time and destroying his clocks, Halliday experiences the perfect fulfillment of his dream, but then, recogniing the destructive, deadly aspect of Gabrielle, he flees from her, from the darkness and the timeless desert, returning to the realm "of light and time" (22).

In the relationship among Halliday, Mallory, and Gabrielle a configuration of characters familiar from earlier fiction by Ballard is clearly distinguishable. The mocking, menacing, white-suited Dr. Mallory, "like a white vampire" (13), is another embodiment of the figure of the anti-self, the shadow, dangerous and equivocal but the possessor of secret knowledge required by the questor, an antagonist to be overcome. Gabrielle Szabo is another incarnation of the figure of the anima or soul-image, the highest aspiration and necessary complement of the psyche, but in this instance she embodies the anima in its malevolent aspect, that of the *femme fatale*. Gabrielle's name suggests resurrection, but as Halliday discovers, it is a resurrection that can only be accomplished through the death of the external personality, the ego-self. Halliday's refusal to accept the full implications of his dream constitutes a denial of his own deepest desires, an act destructive of hope and longing. His is a failed quest, a retreat from the fecund darkness of the unconscious to the harsh, barren light of the rational ego-mind, from the timeless to the finite, and from potential transfiguration to staticity.

The summons from the unconscious is at once more terrible and more irresistible in "Storm Bird, Storm Dreamer."[21] Again, the individual call occurs in the context of a catastrophe which is itself a summons from the collective unconscious, another familiar pattern in Ballard's fiction. In this instance, the disaster is a plague of giant birds, the result of mutations caused by the use of "new growth promoters" (14) in agriculture. The main character of the story, Crispin, may even be said to be responsible, at least in part, for the advent of the giant birds, since at the time that the first new growth-promoter sprays were being utilized, killing thousands of birds as an unforeseen side-effect, Crispin saved many of the victims, whose offspring became the first generation of mutant birds.

Later, Crispin joins the militia formed to combat the "aerial armada of millions of birds" (15) and slaughters many hundreds of them, though not without a sense of regret and disquiet aroused by "their great tragic faces" (14) and their haunting resemblance to "fallen angels" (17). By slow degrees though, he begins to identify himself with the birds, until at last he clothes himself in the hallow carcass of a dead bird and for a brief moment glides through the air inside the bird's body before being shot, having been mistaken for one of the giant birds.

The central image of the story is, of course, that of the giant birds, which despite their destructive nature are depicted in terms of the numinous. They are repeatedly likened to "angels" (17, 22, 27), while at the same time their resemblance to human beings and the human resemblance to birds (cf. the beaked noses of Crispin and Quimby, and the feather-clad woman) are repeatedly suggested. In this way the birds may be seen to represent an apocalyptic force, destructive but purifying, a metaphysical-evolutionary force latent in the human psyche, secretly willed by our unconscious intelligence, but resisted by our ego-identities. Crispin's experience encapsulates the human dilemma in the face of energies from within ourselves that threaten our ego-consciousness: First, Crispin unknowingly helps to create the giant birds, then he denies, resists them; subsequently, however, he begins to undergo an inner metamorphosis, dreaming of birds, perceiving his body in terms of avian anatomy, sensing the emergence of a bird identity from within himself; and, finally, relinquishing his human identity and accepting his identity as a bird. At a symbolic level the story depicts our intense desire for and our terror of psychic metamorphosis, our urgent need to evolve from and to transcend our superficial, finite selves and our fierce resistance to doing so.

Even without our resistance the way to self-discovery and transcendence is arduous and perplexing. There is no accurate map, no clear set of directions to determine the course to be travelled, only a sort of cryptic inner compass or a random and haphazard sense of dead reckoning by which to navigate. This aspect of the quest for identity and transcendence serves to make up the motif of "Journey Across a Crater."[22]

The amnesiac astronaut of the story, survivor of a "space disaster" (2), engaged in a search to recover his "lost space capsule" (3) and his lost identity, which he only dimly recalls, may be seen as a metaphor for the human condition. Out of a seemingly incongruous collection of artefacts, comprising items of an utterly trivial or of a bizarre character, the astronaut attempts to assemble the components of "a propulsion device" (5), the elements of a space vehicle. In a similar manner, we are all the amnesiac victims of an unimaginable disaster of consciousness; we are all ontological castaways and prisoners of the law of gravity. Like the astronaut, we are engaged in a desperate search for means of rescue, striving to discover a mode of propulsion, to construct a vehicle that will achieve escape velocity and return us to our proper element.

The motif of escape by means of flight and that of the extreme difficulty attendant upon the attempt to escape are also central to "My Dream of Flying to Wake Island."[23] The main character of the story, Melville, is also an earthbound astronaut, recuperating after a nervous breakdown, plagued by migraine, and obsessed with the idea of flying to Wake Island. Melville discovers a crashed World War II B-17 bomber buried in the dunes of the beach near his house and he labors to excavate it, dreaming that he will renovate the aircraft and use it to fly to Wake Island. The task proves to be Herculean but Melville persists in the undertaking, sustained by his dream.

The choice of Wake Island for a destination would seem to be significant here, suggesting a realm of awakened life or awareness, in contrast to our somnabular world. For Melville it seems to represent a sort of ontological Eden in that he envisions it as "a zone of intense possibility" where "Once he touched down he knew that his migraines would go away for ever" (125). It is also his belief that "Only Wake has real time" (126), and that it is "a place of beginnings . . . not ends" (130). The aircraft that he finds buried beneath the dunes seems to suggest the potential for transcendence which is buried beneath the surface of our conscious life, in the unconscious, a power that requires excavation and perhaps renovation as well. Melville's dream of flying to Wake Island and his discovery of the buried aircraft represent his personal summons to liberate the energies of the buried self and to employ them in the quest for awakened being.

That the summons from the unconscious to change and to evolve may assume a form so unforeseen and so alien that it inspires horror and disgust and excites the most intense and determined resistance is the subject of "Low-Flying Aircraft."[24] The story concerns a future earth that is almost depopulated and "headed for oblivion within a generation" (95) due to widespread mutation among the newborn. The birth rate itself is soaring, fertility rates are high, but the average for normal births is less than one in one thousand. The mutant children are exterminated quietly and efficiently just after birth by the authorities, with the consent and approval of the parents. These deformed offspring, with their defective eyes, and what is far more disturbing, "their deformed sexual organs," arouse "all kinds of nervousness and loathing" (95), and the notion of allowing them to live is universally considered to be utterly contrary to what is reasonable or desirable.

In fact, a few such mutants do survive in secret and show themselves to be highly intelligent and resourceful; moreover, they are not blind, as is generally supposed, but are instead responding to "a different section of the electromagnetic spectrum" (105). Only one man, Gould, perceives that the unprecedented fertility and intensified sexual drive that have characterized the human race since the advent of the mutation process are misinterpreted or disregarded signs "that we were intended to embark on a huge replacement programme, though sadly the people we're replacing turn out to be ourselves. Our job is simply to repopulate the world with our successors" (106). Gould convinces a young couple not to destroy their newborn mutant child but to hand it over to other adult mutants to be raised by them. In this way the new race will survive to supersede the human race and will inhabit what will literally be a new earth under a new heaven.

The story serves to illustrate how our prejudices and preconceptions, our egocentricity and anthropocentricity, act as impediments to our perception and understanding of vital events. The allusion made in the story by Gould to a "massacre of innocents . . . that literally out-Herods Herod" (102) emphasizes the manner in which our fear and our selfishness or merely our habits of thought lead us to oppose evolutionary advances of whatever nature, both personal and collective, whenever they occur. The mutational extension of perception and sexuality in the new race beyond the limitations of human experience is in keeping with the centrality and interrelatedness of these phenomena throughout Ballard's work.

In "The Ultimate City"[25] the author creates again a myth of psychic integration, once more using *The Tempest* as a sort of imbedded structure, an implicit metaphor for the process of self-realization. The poles of the story are Garden City, one of a number of pastoral, post-technological communities throughout the world; and the old metropolis, a nameless, abandoned city, relic of the age of technology and fossil fuels. Garden City embodies social organization at its most enlightened, constituting a scientifically advanced agrarian society characterized by a non-competitive ethos and a bucolic serenity and gentleness which tend, however, toward a sort of torpor and spiritual inertia; while the old metropolis embodies still the lure of the lurid, the fascination of the forbidden, the fecund energies of the unconscious.

Imagery of flight is prominent in the story. The protagonist, a young man named Halloway, flies from Garden City to the old metropolis by means of a sail plane he has constructed. During his sojourn in the city Halloway dreams recurrently of flight in aircraft made of glass. He ignores his dreams, however, repressing his urge to fly, reactivating instead the old metropolis, its traffic lights, neons, and pinball machines, attracting young settlers from the countryside, and reanimating all the problems of the age of fossil fuels, including pollution, crime, debt, stress, inflation, and urban congestion. In the end, following a nightmare apocalypse of violence and destruction in the streets of the renovated metropolis, Halloway abandons the city and turns again to his dream of flight.

Halloway's journey from his home to the old metropolis represents a journey into his own unconscious, a confrontation with the secret forces of his own psyche. Significantly, when Halloway first arrives in the city, carried there by his sail plane, he collides with his own mirror-image reflected in the mirror-glass side of a skyscraper. His subsequent encounter with the remaining residents of the city may be seen, at a symbolic level, as a confrontation with his own psychic energies: Buckmaster and Olds embodying the creative energies and corresponding to Prospero and Ariel, respectively; Stillman personifying the negative, destructive energies, and corresponding to Caliban; while the highest powers and aspirations of the psyche are embodied in Buckmaster's daughter, Miranda, whose name is identical with that of the character in *The Tempest* with whom she is a parallel.

During the course of his sojourn in the metropolis, Halloway lives out the imperatives of the dark, demonic energies within him, and in the end achieves a readjustment of inner forces and a re-orientation of his life in terms of his goals and values. Halloway's new psychic integration will permit him to devote his full energy to the goal of flight or transcendence, the fulfillment of his original dream.

"The Ultimate City" suggests that utopian communities inevitably become static, monotonous, and spiritually moribund, and that, cut off from the fecundating energies of the unconscious, civilized life withers and atrophies. Human salvation, then, is not to be attained through even the best-intentioned and most advanced forms of social organization. Renewal and transformation, whether individual or collective, the story suggests, must be achieved through a descent into the unknown depths of the psyche, there to discover and assimilate, submit to and subdue the dangerous and equivocal, creative and redemptive powers of the inner world. Only when this adventure has been concluded do we become fully human and truly civilized, and only then can we begin to assist in the great enterprise of existence: the transfiguration and transcendence of the material world.

This ultimate end of consciousness and matter, its ascent to the realm of light eternal, is lyrically imaged in Halloway's dream:

Halloway dreamed that he was standing at an open window overlooking the park. Below him the waist-high grass shivered and seethed. Some deep motion had unsettled the ground, a profound shudder that crossed the entire park. The bushes and brambles, the trees and shrubs, even the lowliest weeds and wild flowers, were beginning to rustle and quiver, straining from the ground. Everywhere branches were waving in an invisible wind, leaves beating at the passing air. Then, by the lake, at the centre of the park, a miniature oak broke free, boughs moving like the wings of an ungainly bird. Shaking the earth from its roots, it soared towards Halloway, a hundred feet from the ground. Other trees were following, branches grasping at the air, a million leaves whirling together. As Halloway watched, gripping the window-sill to stop himself from joining them, the whole park suddenly rose upwards, every tree and flower, every blade of grass joining to form an immense sunlit armada that circled above Halloway's head and soared along the rays of the sun. As they moved across the sky Halloway could see that all over the city the flowers and vines which Miranda had planted were also leaving. A flight of poppies soared past, a crimson carpet followed by an aerial causeway of daisies, petals beating as if they were the cilia of some huge lace-like creature. Halloway looked up from the city, with its now barren stone and dying air. The sky was filled with a legion of flying creatures, a green haze of petals and blossoms free at last to make their way to the welcoming sun. (79–80)

The image of flight as a metaphor for transcendence is also central to "Notes Toward a Mental Breakdown."[26] The main character of the story, Robert Laughlin, is a week-end pilot with an "obsessional" (76) interest in man-powered flight, and in the construction of "conceptual flying machines" (77). As Laughlin begins to undergo a mental breakdown, he becomes increasingly preoccupied with abandoned airfields, visiting one after another, filming their runways. A related fixation is that of constructing "a unique flying machine" in which he and his wife can "fly to some Elysian landing field" (79).

The story's unusual narrative technique, a first-person account written, annotated, and interpreted from a third-person point-of-view, is expressive of the story's central theme of the dividedness of the human psyche: the aspirations of the unconscious mind checked and rejected by the rational, analytical intelligence; while the narrow, banal perceptions and conceptions of quotidian consciousness are, in turn, sabotaged and subverted by irruptions of the unconscious. Laughlin's quotation from Max Ernst summarizes in a pointed and elegant fashion the character of the conflict between these opposing psychic forces:

Voracious gardens in turn devoured by a vegetation which springs from the debris of trapped airplanes. (78)

The motifs of dividedness and of the quest for transcendence are further treated in "Zodiac 2000,"[27] in which the universe itself is seen as divided between two parallel, mirror-image universes, the one (ours) with a right-hand bias, and the other, unknown, universe with a left-hand bias. The unnamed protagonist of the story, a long-term patient in a mental institution, is discovered to have been "born from a mirror universe, propelled into our own world by cosmic forces of unlimited power" (67). Released from the mental hospital into the custody of a group of scientists for purposes of testing and experimentation, the man escapes, soon thereafter to be taken prisoner by a group of terrorists, from whom he also contrives to escape, only to be caught by the police and returned to the mental institution. But this fugitive from another universe possesses the capacity to transcend our universe, and as the story ends he is preparing to effect his ultimate escape: "Now he would leave them, and take the left-handed staircase to the roof above his mind, and fly away across the free skies of his inner space" (75).

"Zodiac 2000" may be read as a symbolic statement concerning the human predicament, inasmuch as we are all, in a metaphoric sense, fugitives from another, better universe, strangers to this continuum of time and space, prisoners of matter and of "this nightmare world of terrorists and cruise missiles" (73). Likewise, in common with the institutionalized protagonist of the story, we all possess, latent in the psyche, the capacity for transcendence, the ability to disengage ourselves from this plane of being and to attain to a higher level of consciousness. Like the fugitive/prisoner of the story, we can all, with enough determination, fly away across the free skies of inner space.

In a series of three closely related stories Ballard explores the possibility of the activation of our latent powers and the realization of our desire to transcend our ego-identities and the limits of our physical, temporal world. With their obvious parallels, correspondences, and overlapping motifs, the three stories may be seen to represent mutually reflective versions of a single psychic myth.

In the first of the three stories, "News from the Sun,"[28] the awakening of the psyche's latent powers manifests itself in the form of a sort of psychological virus whose metaphysical potential is at first unrecognized. The "time sickness," as the phenomenon is called, causes temporary lapses of consciousness, lapses which increase in interval and in length until the condition becomes permanent. As a consequence of this malaise the technological, civilized world is in a state of dereliction and decay, as gradually every form of commerce and service and every facility and institution ceases to function.

Yet, as a few humans come to realize, the fugues of the time-sickness represent "a way out of time" (83) and "a sign that some great biological step forward is about to take place" (99). Training themselves to remain conscious during the fugues, they discover that they are able to enter a timeless "real world" (110), a "realm of wonder" (111) beyond "the world of appearances" (111) that we normally inhabit. Characteristic of this transcendent realm is brilliant illumination, intense color and paradisical imagery of forests, flowers, verdant valleys, lakes, and streams. The mode of seeing and being induced by the fugues constitutes an ontological Eden: "Everything seemed calm and yet vivid, the young earth seen for the first time, where all . . . ills would be soothed and assuaged in its sweet waters" (108).

We recognize here a pattern familiar from Ballard's earlier disaster tales, that of the catastrophe, which in actuality represents an opportunity to achieve the highest goal and final end of consciousness: union with the infinite. Imagery of the sun, of flight and light, together with the element of eroticism as a catalyst to and an analogue of mystical perception, further serve to unite the story with earlier tales of transcendence. But in "News of the Sun" and its two sister stories, the twin motifs of catastrophe and transcendence attain their most powerful and lyrical expression in Ballard's short fiction, and their fullest development apart from their treatment in the novel *The Unlimited Dream Company*.

In the second of the three stories, "Memories of the Space Age,"[29] the quest for an ontological Eden is undertaken by Dr. Mallory and his wife, Anne, who have journeyed to the abandoned towers and derelict runways of Cape Kennedy, drawn there by recurrent dreams and guided by some inner compass. The Mallorys were once employed by NASA and they have returned "like Adam and Eve" (4), as we are told, to the overgrown jungles of Florida as fugitives from "the space sickness" (4), a malady that affects consciousness in much the same way as the "time sickness" of the preceeding story, causing lapses of consciousness which are of increasing frequency and duration. The "space sickness" is also responsible for widespread mutation among newborn children, who are afflicted by mongolism and autism, "diseases of time, malfunctions to the temporal sense" (4). The Mallorys are convinced that the key to the space sickness is to be found at Cape Kennedy.

The key to the disease is incarnate in the figure of Hinton, an ex-astronaut and an escaped murderer, who alone perceives the meaning of the space sickness, its function as an egress from the world of time. As Mallory observes of him: "he seems to have embraced the destruction of time, as if this whole malaise were an opportunity that we ought to seize, the next evolutionary step forward" (11). Ultimately, inspired and guided by Hinton, Mallory and Anne also learn to embrace the disease as a form of grace, and as a consequence of so doing they experience the transfiguration of the material, temporal world as a prelude to their final entry into a timeless realm of pure light and pure being beyond the finite, physical world. The Mallorys learn that the time sickness constitutes a new mode of perception and of consciousness through which they are able to repossess the "primeval paradise" of "a world without time, an indefinite and unending present" (4), and to re-enter the "Eden" (4, 11) of ultimate fulfillment and liberation.

Hinton, who combines the attributes of a mystic with those of a thug, embodies the dual energies of the unconscious, the destructive and the creative, the demonic and the numinous. In him the urge for transcendence is paramount; he has become an agency of the appetite for the infinite, impatient with all encumbrances or impediments, unrestrained by social or moral considerations in his single-minded pursuit of "true flight" (10), that is the flight of the "spiritual body" (11). Hinton recognizes that all other forms of aeronautics, including space flight, are no more than metaphors for the "pure form of flight . . . absolute flight" (11) which is our deepest desire and our real goal.

The last in the series of the three interrelated stories treating the theme of transcendence is "Myths of the Near Future."[30] Again, the location is the Floridian jungle near Cape Kennedy, and again a global catastrophe—one very much along the lines of those in the preceeding two stories—is in progress: an epidemic of the "space sickness," a psychological malady whose bizarre symptoms include the conviction on the part of the victims that "they had once been astronauts . . . had once travelled through space" (13). The terminal stages of the illness consist of complete catatonic withdrawal followed eventually by cessation of all vital physical functions: "All of them, in their last seconds of consciousness, became calm and serene, and murmured like drowsy passengers at the start of a new voyage, their journey home to the sun" (13).

Sheppard, the protagonist of the story, is a man in the early stages of the illness, who is attempting to locate his ex-wife, Elaine, whose illness is at a more advanced stage. He believes she has been abducted by Martinsen, her doctor. As the symptoms of his illness begin to manifest themselves with increasing intensity and frequency, Sheppard discovers that the malady represents "a side-door for all of us to escape through . . . a chance to escape into a world beyond time" (33). In contrast to the luminous, numinous realm he inhabits during the active episodes of the space sickness—the seizures or fugues that it occasions—the quotidian world is experienced by Sheppard as "humdrum" and as a "grey, teased out zone" (29). As a further effect of the illness, Sheppard senses an inner transformation of himself into a glowing, winged man, and when at last he succeeds in freeing Elaine from the cage where she has been kept as a prisoner, she too is "sheathed in light . . . a winged woman" (41). Both Sheppard and Elaine have been liberated from serial, sequential time and have entered a timeless dimension where past, present, and future occur simultaneously. Together, they set off to awaken and to liberate the rest of humanity: "to the sleepwalking children in the parks, to the dreaming mothers and fathers embalmed in their homes, waiting to be woken from the present into the infinite realm of their time-filled selves" (43).

Sheppard's duel against Martinsen to liberate Elaine from her captivity possesses resonances that suggest the struggle of the unconscious against the limiting ego-mind to liberate the spirit. Martinsen is terrified by Elaine's transformation and seeks to keep her confined in order to prevent the further unfolding of her metamorphosis. Rather than embracing the miraculous and the marvelous, he resists it determinedly, attempting to restrict its power by means of various stratagems and subterfuges, all of which prove futile. In the end, Sheppard and Elaine, formerly divorced, are joined together again, constituting in their new union an irresistible liberating force. In this manner, the story may be seen to represent both an allegory of psychic integration and a myth of transcendence.

The recurrent imagery of trapped aircraft and of abandoned airfields, runways and launch pads in "News from the Sun," "Memories of the Space Age," and "Myths of the Near Future" serves to represent humankind's thwarted, neglected potential for flight, that is for the pure flight of the spirit, for transcendence. The ultimate consequence of the frustration and disregard for so deep-seated and intense an urge is the psychological malaise that assumes a similar form in each of the stories. The disease compels us to acknowledge our impotence before the unknown and invisible powers of the world, and to perceive the transience, uncertainty, and limitation of the material-temporal sphere. Moreover, the disease acts as a psychic catalyst, activating latent energies that enable us to achieve true flight and attain to light, to the source and ground of all being and consciousness. The ambient imagery of the three stories consists essentially of two opposing clusters of images: those such as dust, sand and vegetation, rust and decay, that symbolize the entropic processes of the material, temporal world; and those of a spiritual character, including angels, Pentecost, paradise, Eve, Adam, and the Garden of Eden, that represent a higher dimension of being. The author's repeated development and elaboration of this essential configuration suggests its centrality in his imagination.

It will be remembered that in "Myths of the Near Future" one of the symptoms of the space sickness was the conviction formed by the victims of the malady that they had once been astronauts; this conviction, with its metaphoric possibiliites, constitutes the primary motif of "The Man Who Walked on the Moon."[31] The unnamed narrator of the story, a former journalist for a minor newspaper in a small South American country, firmly believes that he was once an astronaut. This conviction is fundamental to his identity and to his mode of life. The narrator has, as it were, inherited the belief and the role from an American named Scranton, a failed crop-duster pilot who conceived and maintained, in the face of all evidence to the contrary and even despite public exposure and ridicule, the notion that he had once been an astronaut, and had once walked upon the lunar surface.

At an earlier period the narrator formed a close association with the imposter Scranton, and under his tutelage awoke to the role of astronaut, learning at first to observe the world through the eyes of Scranton, to project inner silence upon the clamor of the streets, inner light and space upon the thronged and shabby city, learning detachment from life and from time. Through these exercises the narrator gradually becomes "aware of a previous career, which . . . the pressures of everyday life had hidden from me" (33), that is, of course, his previous career as an astronaut. Upon Scranton's death, the narrator assumes in full the role of former astronaut, convinced that his previous life and professional career as a reporter constitute a form of "acute amnesia" (22) and that he has at last realized and regained his "true history and worth" (22).

In a manner similar to the amnesiac astronaut of "Journey Across a Crater" or the cosmic exile of "Zodiac 2000," the narrator of "The Man Who Walked on the Moon" (and his precursor, Scranton) may be seen to represent all of us, in the sense that, figuratively speaking, we are all suffering from "acute amnesia" and must recover the sense of our "true history and worth." For we are all very much reduced and diminished, distorted and deformed versions of what we could be and should be, and indeed, of what we truly and essentially *are*, what we remain beneath or beyond the exterior ego-self. Moreover, again in a metaphorical sense, we may all be said to be former astronauts in that we feel that once (in a pre-existent state, in the womb or as infants) we inhabited an ontological Eden, that once we possessed a mode of consciousness—visionary, mystical, transcendental—which we have lost or forfeited to our culture-conditioned habits of conception and perception. To recognize, as does the narrator of the story and his friend Scranton, that we are former astronauts could represent a first vital step toward the recovery of our original, authentic identity, the regaining of true being.

In this sense, Ballard's later fiction comes thematically full circle, from the revelation of the illusory nature of what is commonly accepted as reality or truth, to the affirmation of the truth of what is generally held to be illusion. The separate stories of this period further extend and elaborate the essential, underlying myth or metaphysic of the author's fiction: the struggle that is enacted both in the microcosm and in the macrocosm between the redintegrative forces of the psyche and all that serves to estrange the psyche from the realization of its identity. These stories repugn and repudiate the world of appearances, the world of time, space, and ego-identity, together with all the various props and agencies of these illusions, and they uphold instead other and higher orders of truth and reality: the invisible world, the truth of imagination, the realm of awakened and infinite being.

5

Release: *The Unlimited Dream Company, Hello America, Empire of the Sun, The Day of Creation, Running Wild*

The clearest exposition and fullest resolution of the theme of transcendence in Ballard's work occurs in his novel, *The Unlimited Dream Company*.[1] In contrast to the cataclysms of the disaster tales with their visions of violence and illness, decay, and destruction, *The Unlimited Dream Company* portrays what is essentially a peaceful, affirmative, and finally joyous metamorphosis, though one that is no less radical in its repudiation of material reality, nor less extensive in its revelatory import. Also, in distinction to nearly all of the author's previous treatments of this theme, in *The Unlimited Dream Company* the quest for transcendence is no longer an isolated individual undertaking, but is rather, by its very nature, a collective human endeavor.

Aside, however, from these distinctions and developments, *The Unlimited Dream Company* employs motifs and images familiar from the earlier stories and novels. Most significant here are Ballard's use of images of light and flight, erotic and spiritual metaphors, Edenic imagery, and shadow and anima figures. The novel represents an integration and a culmination of Ballard's vision, and it is his most mythic, most explicitly metaphysical, most directly allegorical work.

Blake, the protagonist of *The Unlimited Dream Company*, is a young man who in the span of only a few days is transformed from a socially-rejected outsider—one who has been expelled from half-a-dozen schools, thrown out of medical school; a "rejected would-be pilot, failed Jesuit novice, unpublished writer of pornography" (13)—into a messianic figure of enormous charisma and supernatural power. His metamorphosis occurs as a result of his physical death, that is, the liberation of his true self from his corporeal self. Through his acquired powers Blake, in turn, effects the transformation of the placid English town of Shepperton, a sterile, suffocating "paradigm of nowhere" (35), into "a reconditioned Eden" (128), fertile, beauteous, and innocent, and he delivers the inhabitants of the town from their dull and circumscribed lives in the material world into the radiance and ecstasy of true being.

Blake's role is that of an archetypal savior or redeemer, with many parallels to Christ, including miraculous cures, eventual rejection by those whom he has come to save, abuse and humiliation, death and resurrection, and the promise of a second coming. Blake is, at the same time, a very pagan figure, a primitive fertility deity for whom erotic desire is a key to spiritual transformation. And, lastly, he is the incarnation of a mythical, primordial winged man, an original and final man, of whom we are all the fallen descendants; and to this form we shall again evolve.

The central focus of the novel is the inner evolution of Blake, as he gradually comes to comprehend the nature and purpose of the powers he possesses. In the beginning he wishes only to escape from Shepperton and exercises his powers to that end, not scrupling to exploit the inhabitants of the town in the secret pursuit of his goal. After his second death and resurrection, however, Blake becomes selfless and benevolent, sacrificing his own interests for the well-being of others.

In this sense Blake represents a significant evolvement from the rather more insular, self-involved figures of the earlier novels and stories. In contrast to Ballard's earlier protagonists, Blake achieves communion and full mutuality with the human community as well as with the natural world. There is a reciprocal relationship between Blake as messiah and the inhabitants of Shepperton, his congregation. He infuses them with motive and power, while they, in turn, sustain and revitalize him. Capable of ultimate love, self-denial, and unconditional forgiveness, Blake may be seen to represent the first truly whole, truly heroic figure in Ballard's oeuvre.

The conflict and the ultimate integration of forces within Blake's psyche, his inner struggle from self-division to wholeness, is reflected in his relationship to two central figures in the story: Miriam St. Cloud and Stark. The former, as her surname suggests, may be seen to embody the higher aspirations of the psyche, the spiritual impulses, the desire for transcendence, the appetite for the infinite; while the latter personifies the lower urges for pleasure, power, and material possession.

Miriam is an elusive presence in the book, a nurturing and innocent ideal woman who serves both to inspire Blake in the exercise of his miraculous powers and to check his unenlightened, misjudged impulses, such as his compulsion to throttle his lovers in order to liberate them from the confinement of physical being. The final marriage of Miriam and Blake in the air (recalling that of Sheppard and Elaine in "Myths of the Near Future") is symbolic of their complete union, the ultimate merging of self and spirit, and of their consequent release from the laws of the physical world. The larger dimension of symbolism suggested by their marriage will be discussed below.

Significantly, it is Stark who seeks to prevent that marriage. He also leads the revolt of the townspeople against the reign of the miraculous and the marvelous instituted by Blake. Throughout the story Stark acts as a counter-force, an anti-self to Blake, resisting and sabotaging the transcendental desires embodied by Blake because he fears to lose the pleasures and satisfactions of his limited world. While everyone else in Shepperton is joyously relinquishing money and material possessions for the ecstasies of the erotico-spiritual, Stark is busily and greedily gathering as much loot as he can carry. He continually attempts to undermine Blake's role as redeemer, even raising the drowned Cessna in order to confront Blake with the irrefutable fact of his physical death in the hope of thereby destroying his powers. Appropriately, Stark keeps a small zoo—symbolic of the confinement and oppression of the instincts, of sexuality and desire, and of all impulses to freedom. Likewise, he runs a small Ferris wheel, a metaphor for the restraint and perversion of the desire to ascend, to fly. Suggestively, too, Stark drives a hearse and keeps vultures, both indicative of his role as "the death angel" (188), slayer of Blake and Miriam and eradicator of all manifestations of the marvelous and the ethereal.

In addition to his struggle with Stark, Blake is involved in a "duel" (94) with his dead corporeal self, the drowned body still seated at the controls of the Cessna at the bottom of the river. Again and again, by day and at night in his dreams, Blake is drawn back to the submerged aircraft to confront the dead pilot, his former self, and to evade its embrace. Once in a park, he finds himself re-enacting the "titanic underwater combat, wrestling with myself" (49); on another occasion, he suddenly beholds "the dead pilot in his ragged flying suit . . . come ashore to find me" (116). This recurrent conflict with his dead self is emblematic of the struggle of the true self or spirit with the physical self, which stubbornly attempts to maintain or to re-establish its hegemony. A further manifestation of the conflict may be seen in the clothes Blake dons after the crash to replace his pilot apparel: a black suit "of a priest or funeral mute" (32)—attire appropriate either to transcendence or to death.

This conflict, in all its metaphysical significance, derives from Blake's imperfect liberation from his body image and ego-consciousness, and the consequent persistence of a sense of identity with his external, material self. The effect of this unresolved struggle is to impede the complete unfolding of Blake's powers. In the end, though, as a result of his second death and resurrection, he is freed from all such residual doubts and lingering fears. He is able to confront with complete indifference the raised aircraft which Stark has spitefully retrieved from the river, and to absorb his own skeleton, merge with, and transfigure his death, transmuting it into new life and new energy. Blake learns to affirm the new life, the life of the spirit, which can fully be realized only through physical death. In equal measure, he learns to disdain that physical life which implies the death of the spirit; he chooses the role of priest over that of funeral mute.

In order fully and finally to transcend the realm of time and space and to attain to an ontological Eden, Blake—together with the inhabitants of Shepperton—must pass through a sequence of alchemical transformations, through the elements of air, water, earth, and fire. The first three transformations are successfully achieved, but Blake balks at the final, transfiguring metamorphois, the "communion of light" (162), the journey to the sun. In fear of annihilation Blake resists this ultimate consummation. Only after his second death does he comprehend the joy and beauty of such a consummation, absolute union with "the sea of light that formed the universre" (223), the fulfillment and the exaltation of all time, matter, life, and consciousness in "the last marriage of the animate and the inanimate, of the living and the dead" (223).

Ballard's essential metaphysic, as it is expressed in *The Unlimited Dream Company*, has obvious affinities with elements of Neo-Platonism and of Eastern spiritual traditions. The material world, the realm of physical existence as perceived by the senses, is seen as an inferior, even illusory level of being, a fallen world. There is an innate urge in the psyche to return to the realm of true and unified being, the ultimate and ideal world, which exists utterly beyond what we mistakenly perceive as reality. Dreams, desire, the unconscious mind, visionary and sur-rational states are gateways to the Absolute, as are love and forgiveness, since they transcend ego-consciousness, and are—as William Blake believed—the highest expressions of the imagination.

The central metaphor used by Ballard in the novel to represent the relationshp between the two realms of being is that of an advent calendar: "Each leaf was a shutter about to swing back and reveal a miniature sun, one window in the immense advent calendar of nature" (88); and "I could release the light waiting behind the shutter of reality each of them bore before him like a shield" (82); and "the real world that waited behind the shutter of every flower and feather, every leaf and child" (93).

The impediments that separate us from the timeless realm of the absolute, keeping us on this side of the advent calendar, are embodied in the novel by the characters of the three handicapped orphans, Rachel, David, and Jamie, whose blindness, lameness, and mongolism represent the perceptual, physical, and intellectual limitations that prevent us from discovering the paradise that lies both within ourselves and everywhere about us, just beyond the reach of our consciousness.

The author employs recurrent images of sleeping and waking, death and life to express the states of being in the material world and in transcendent reality. The townspeople of Shepperton, in Blake's transforming presence, are "sleepers waking from their long dream" (159). And, as Father Wingate remarks to Blake: "it was not death you survived but life . . . it's not you who are alive but we here who are dead" (79). The images of light and of flight that are so central to the novel (as to nearly all of Ballard's fiction) culminate in the final apocalypse of the story as metaphors of unified and absolute being: "the infinitely chambered heart of the great bird of which we were all part" (222), and the sun toward which the merged inhabitants of Shepperton ascend, "the sea of light" (223), which is the first and last, the perennial and eternal ground of all being.

Something of the dramatic appeal and the poetic resonance of *The Unlimited Dream Company* may be said to derive from the novel's correspondences with mythic patterns and sacred traditions, including those of the redeemer, death and rebirth, the sacred marriage, and paradise. Blake's role in the novel may be compared to that of figures such as Dionysus and Orpheus in classical mythology in that he brings to the community fecundating power and power over birds, beasts and fishes, plants and trees; he imparts ecstasies and instigates orgiastic rites, and serves as conduit to a divine or transpersonal reality. Like Orpheus or Osiris, Blake is a sacrificial figure who undergoes death and dismemberment for the spiritual elevation or redemption of the community, and like them he overcomes death and is reborn.

The resolution of contrarieties, the union of opposites is imaged in the novel by the archetype of sacred marriage (between Miriam and Blake), a metaphor for the restoration of divided, fragmented creation to original unity. Blake's transformation of Shepperton to a lush, fertile earthly paradise is likewise symbolic of the restoration of the fallen world to its prelapsarian innocence and primordial wholeness; while the journey to the sun, symbol of the source of all being, represents the return of human consciousness to the highest paradise: union with the Infinite. In this manner, the novel may seen to constitute a contemporary reinterpretation and renewal of some of the most archaic and most universal of our collective dreams, as expressed in ancient myth and symbol.

Patterns of myth and archetype also inform Ballard's next novel, *Hello America*,[2] including those of the search for the father, the quest for the Promised Land or Earthly Paradise, the archetype of the redeemer, and the myth of the Wasteland. The novel not only re-interprets these myths but employs them as a basis from which to address the question of the nature of myth and its function with regard to the processes of perception and conceptualization and of human evolution.

Hello America is set approximately 130 years in the future and concerns a scientific expedition sent from Europe to the long-abandoned and climatically devastated continent of North America. A little more than 100 years previous to the arrival of the expedition an energy crisis of major dimensions and the consequent collapse of the U.S. economy combined to drive Americans from their homeland, and in a reverse migration, to seek refuge in the countries of Europe, Africa, and Asia. Subsequent geo-engineering, climatic control measures undertaken to promote agriculture in other areas of the globe, transformed the landscape of the uninhabited American continent into two regions: a vast desert and a dense tropical rain forest. By coincidence, each member of the expedition sent from Europe to America is descended from American forebears, and many have been raised within American exile communities.

The protagonist of the novel, a young man named Wayne, has crossed the Atlantic as a stowaway aboard the expedition's ship. He has come to America in search of his father, Dr. William Flemming, who vanished during an expedition to the American interior twenty years earlier, and also because he is obsessed with all the legends and myths of the American past. Described as a "young redeemer" (84), Wayne secretly hopes somehow to reinvigorate the moribund land, to "make it bloom again" (50) and "to irrigate the desert in all senses" (87). In the tradition of generations of immigrants to the American shore, Wayne dreams of becoming President of the United States.

To Wayne, America still retains in a dormant, latent form its once potent magic, and he views as "the real purpose of the expedition— the attempt to find that special 'America' inside each one of us" (93). The essential, informing myth of America, as Wayne apprehends it, is the exploration of the imperatives of the self: "The United States had based itself on the proposition that everyone should be able to live out his furthest fantasies, wherever they might lead, explore every opportunity, however bizarre" (106). In this sense, the expedition's journey inland and westward across the empty, arid landscape represents for each of its members a journey inward, a quest for identity and for a renewal of purpose, for a sense of orientation and direction in life.

The America of *Hello America* is at once the Promised Land and the Wasteland; that is, it constitutes a blighted paradise, a promised land laid waste and under a curse. The cause of the land's desolation lies in the failure of its inhabitants to maintain faith in the myth, the dream of America. During the energy and economic crises of the late twentieth century, "the whole nation seemed to lose its vitality, its belief in itself and its future" (46). Their forsaking of the dream and their abandonment of the land resulted in the devastation of the once fertile continent. Wayne ultimately succeeds in redeeming the dream of America when he ceases to mistake the outworn outward forms of the myth for its essence and inner meaning, that is, when he learns to distinguish myth from illusion.

The process by which Wayne learns to discriminate between myth and illusion begins just after landfall on the American shore. Viewed from a distance at sea, the city of New York appears to be covered with gold, the literal manifestation of the old metaphor, but upon closer inspection the golden sheen proves to be compounded of dust and rust. Subsequently, Wayne is also misled by illusions such as those of laser-projected images, of automatons in the form of legendary American figures, and of the dazzle and glamour of a miniature America resurrected in Las Vegas by a psychopath who has taken the name of Charles Manson and the title of President of the United States.

Manson embodies the false father, as well as the Father of Lies, in contrast to Dr. Flemming, who is Wayne's true father in both a literal and a figurative sense. For a long period of time Wayne is deceived by Manson, believing that Manson shares with him a common vision of America, of its potential and its historical significance, but ultimately he discovers that their visions of America are antithetical. In another sense, Manson represents a sort of Fisher King figure, the ruler of the Wasteland whose wound causes its infertility and desolation. Manson's wound is his belief in illusion, his quest for temporal power rather than for redeeming vision, his drive toward death rather than life. Manson's fundamental perceptual and spiritual error is that he mistakes image for substance, external form for internal significance. We first see Manson in his sterilized hotel suite (formerly occupied by Howard Hughes, upon whose character that of Manson is modelled in part) sitting naked amid rows of television screens and walls of photographs, at once a potentate and a prisoner of image and illusion: "His eyes were fixed on the tiers of screens, as if his real existence resided in the ionised flow of flickering images . . ." (127); and, "The images glimmered away, lighting up Manson's pallid skin, a ghostly second epidermis. On the walls behind him was a display of framed photographs, old news agency pictures from the middle and late twentieth century" (129).

In the end, Wayne frees himself from Manson's mad, messianic spell, the ultimate American illusion. Wayne rejects Manson's America of gunships and missiles, of technology and power, for the transcendent vision of his natural father, Dr. Flemming, who constructs sun-powered aeroplanes of thinnest glass, to fly to "the morning gardens of the West" (222) and thence to the sun. Manson and Flemming externalize Wayne's inner conflict, his struggle between the attractions of power and vision, glamour and self-realization, illusion and myth. Wayne's final resolution of this conflict occurs in such a manner as to help precipitate the collapse of Manson's empire and the redemption and renewal of the dream of America: "The old dreams were dead, Manson and Mickey Mouse and Marilyn Monroe belonged to a past America . . . It was time for new dreams, worthy of a real tomorrow" (224).

The experience of the expedition from landfall to Las Vegas recapitulates in miniature the history of the American nation: immigration, westward expansion, encounters with indigenous peoples, rise to prosperity, the ascendance of technology, the acquisition of an atomic arsenal, and the achievement of status as a world power. In addition, various members of the expedition adopt roles of American archetypes: the cowboy, the gangster, the glamour girl, the eccentric genius-inventor, the Horatio Alger type of young-man-of-humble-origins who acquires wealth and prestige through diligence and ambition. And Manson, too, embodies an American archetype: the dark side of the American dream, the paranoid, the messianic psychopath obsessed with power and with the destruction of his enemies, a strain of megalomania that manifests itself in the various tycoons and minor tyrants throughout the American experience who confused power and prosperity with freedom, mistook license for liberty and appearance for reality, who propagated falsehood in place of truth, and perpetrated destruction in place of creation. In this sense, too, American history repeats itself in the novel, for Manson's failure "to protect and defend the constitution of the United States" according to the oath of the office which he has usurped, his essential inability to perceive a reality beyond the parameters of his paranoia, leads once again to the destruction of the resurrected American nation.

In the context of the novel, the American myth represents the last hope to revive an exhausted Europe with its "interminable rationing and subsistence living, its total lack of any flair and opportunity" (9), and to reinvigorate and renew a world dominated by necessity, with no room for fantasy or freedom. As Wayne recognizes, a resurrected America, even on a small scale, represents "a node of intense possibility that could expand to transform the planet, start everything up again" (132). The end of Manson's rule constitutes a major step toward such a renascent America. The remaining barrier is that of the Bering Straits Dam which is responsible for the climactic changes that have been wrought upon the American continent. The dam may be seen as a metaphor for the blockage of psychic energy that has brought the world of the twenty-first century to such a pass. The dam obstructs the energy that should by rights flow to America—emblematic in the novel of imagination and freedom—thereby rendering it infertile; and the dam diverts that energy to arctic regions, a geographic metaphor suggesting the realm of rationality and practicality, the dreamless, demythicized world of utilitarian values.

Likewise, in our scientific-technological culture, the energies that should be directed to the exploration of the unconscious, to the cultivation of the faculties of imagination and vision, have instead been dammed and diverted to irrigate the rational, analytical intelligence. A consequence of this unnatural deflection of energy is our declining ability to understand the vital language of myth and symbol. All too often we fail to comprehend the very nature of symbol and myth: that they are vehicles of meaning, media of metaphoric truth, and are not to be taken as being true in a literal sense. Indeed, to understand them in this manner and at this level is to misundertand them entirely. Myth must not be apprehended—as does Manson in the novel—as fixed and final. Such an attitude serves to arrest the processes of inner growth and transformation that symbol and myth should engender.

Myths and symbols may more properly be understood as tentative organizations of energy and impulse, as living shapes, organic, protean, fluid, and not as changeless and absolute structures. If regarded in a rigid, literal sense, if made the basis for some reductive orthodoxy, then the living myth and the fecund symbol become inert, withering into illusion, serving then to stifle and repress the process of change and growth rather than to promote it.

The failure of America, as embodied chiefly in the character of Manson in the novel, is that of forsaking and denying the spirit, the true substance and significance of myth, by upholding only the outer form of the myth, its mere husk, its petrified shell. Thus, the task of the redeemer-hero, Wayne, is to release the original, inform-ing energy of the myth from its narrow captivity so that it may assume a new form, express itself in new symbols and myths. Wayne succeeds in so doing and the concluding images of the novel depict the rebirth of the American myth as the children of America fly westward and sunward on their glass aeroplanes in the morning light, and Wayne dreams of becoming "the first of the Presidents of the Sunlight Fliers" (224).

The theme of illusion is also central to Ballard's next novel, *Empire of the Sun*.[3] Here, the emphasis is upon the process by which events, ideas, and emotions become distorted and falsified through their expression as cinematic, photographic, or linguistic images. The process is completed when the human mind, in turn, absorbs these misrepresentations, accepting them at their face value, so that they come to constitute a sort of inner screen according to which reality is perceived and interpreted. The end result is a state of collective illusion and of perpetual conflict based upon the collision and competition of unlike and incompatible illusions.

The chief focus of the operation of this process of illusion in *Empire of the Sun* is the British business and administrative community, together with their dependents, in Shanghai, China during the period 1941 to 1945, or from just before to just after the war with Japan. The specific narrative focus of the story is the character of Jim, who is eleven years old when the war breaks out. He becomes separated from his family and is interned by the Japanese together with other foreign nationals in Lunghua Camp for the duration of the war. The camp is the novel's central metaphor for the fixedness and enclosure—imposed from without and self-imposed—of the reductive or deliberately deceptive im-age, the internalized falsehood which is the basic unit of illusion.

Jim is one of the very few characters in the novel to perceive the disparity between image and reality, and to attempt to conduct himself accordingly. Dr. Ransome notes this ability and praises Jim for not confusing "the map with the territory" (97). Already before the outbreak of the war with Japan, Jim is aware of the incongruity of the newsreels of the European war, which are being shown repeatedly all over Shanghai, with the actual scenes of war which he has witnessed between the Chinese and Japanese forces in the countryside just outside of Shanghai. At night Jim's dreams take the form of silent scenes of battle, "as if his sleeping mind was trying to separate the real war from the make-believe conflicts invented by Pathé and British Movietone" (5). In contrast to the simplistic, pre-digested, patriotic commentaries of the newsreel war, Jim notes that "Real war was the thousands of Chinese refugees dying of cholera in the sealed stockades at Pootung, and the bloody heads of the communist soldiers mounted on pikes along the Bund. In a real war no one knew which side he was on, and there were no flags or commentators or winners. In a real war there were no enemies" (5–6). Despite his precocious insights into the nature of real war, the problem of distinguishing between image and reality, between falsehood and truth, is one that occupies Jim throughout the novel.

In a sense, the interned British nationals of the novel merely exchange one form of confinement for another, inasmuch as the insular, culturally hermetic community of the International Settlement constitutes a species of self-imposed imprisonment hardly less limiting in its way than the Lunghua Camp. In a similar manner, the inmates of the camp may be said to have exchanged one form of privation for another, trading the slow starvation of the spirit, heart and intellect attendant upon residence in the International Settlement for the slow starvation of the body in the internment camp. And, common to both forms of confinement are the invisible enclosing walls made up of the habits of perception and conceptualization with which the prisoners have been inculcated by their culture, and the restraining fetters forged of the abstractions, stereotypes, and clichés that they have inherited and have accepted without question.

During the four years of their captivity at Lunghua Camp, the British inmates grow increasingly demoralized and passive. Their psychic energies are consumed by futile attempts to deny or evade the reality of their situation. They cling desperately to familiar forms or retreat into memory or fantasy. One tactic of evasion is that of the signposting of the pathways of the camp, naming them after the streets of London. As Jim remarks: "Naming the sewage-stained paths between the rotting huts after a vaguely remembered London allowed too many of the British prisoners to shut out the reality of the camp, another excuse to sit back when they should have been helping Dr. Ransome to clear the septic tanks" (129).

Another tactic is that of nostalgic reverie such as indulged in by Mrs. Vincent who stares for hours at the blank wall of her cubicle, watching an "invisible film" (133) of pre-war England projected by her memory. Even the energetic Dr. Ransome assigns Jim Latin lessons, largely in order to sustain the illusion "that even in Lunghua Camp the values of a vanished England still survived" (147), while Mr. Maxted attempts to curb Jim's offbeat philosophizing by admonishing him: "Remember you're British" (184). But neither Latin grammar nor appeals to national pride are effective in the least in preventing Jim from perceiving the realities of the camp as they exist behind the inmates' collective facade of sentimentality and stiff-upper-lip-ism: the stark, immitigable facts of disease, hunger, fear, and death, of acts of casual cruelty, of cynicism, and selfish indifference to the needs and lives of others.

The long-term result of the confinement of the inmates of Lunghua Camp is that not only do the prisoners make no attempt to escape but they actually assist their captors in strengthening the fences of the camp in order to keep out the starving Chinese. Moreover, following their "liberation" at the end of the war, several hundred former prisoners return to the camp to take up residence in fear of the chaotic conditions prevailing outside the fences of the camp. Our habits, the author suggests, are dearer to us by far than our freedom, and comfortable illusions so much more congenial to us than the insecurities and challenges of the quest for truth.

Throughout the story Jim is alternately provoked and compelled to separate truth from illusion. Beginning with the first seeds of doubt sewn already before the outbreak of the war with Japan, Jim's internal process of learning to discern and to discriminate is, of necessity, much accelerated by the advent of the war which results in his initial isolation and his subsequent prolonged captivity. The war effectively shatters Jim's identity together with all his received values and notions of life, and forces him to reconstruct himself from the ground up, as it were.

The break-up of Jim's personality is imaged in a series of reflections in fractured mirrors. When Jim returns home shortly after the breakup of hostilities, he views his image in the newly broken mirror in his mother's bedroom in which "pieces of himself seemed to fly across the room," and in which he appears as "a small exploding boy" (44). At first, Jim desperately denies the reality of the war, attempting to pretend that nothing has changed, and thus to hold "at bay the deformed figure in the fractured mirror" (45), but already within a few days' time his face begins to assume "a tighter and older shape" (54), and soon thereafter that of "an urchin half his previous size and twice his previous age" (60). Jim acquires both a new name (having been called "Jamie" before) and a new perspective on life: "he knew now that kindness, which his parents and teachers had always urged upon him, counted for nothing" (62). Ultimately, following his internment at the Shanghai Central Prison and then in the detention center, Jim discovers that: "when he looked at himself in the cracked glass panes of the ticket kiosk, he barely remembered the long face with its deep eye-sockets and bony forehead" (83). From this point forward Jim avoids mirrors, and it is at this stage of his metamorphosis that he becomes aware that "Parts of his mind and body frequently separated themselves from each other" (84).

Jim's new divided, dissociated self is reflected in his two new mentors: Basie and Dr. Ransome. Basie, an American merchant seaman, a mess steward, is an amoral, self-seeking manipulator, a shameless, ruthless opportunist dedicated fully and exclusively to his own survival. As his name suggests he is both basic and base. Dr. Ransome, on the other hand, is compassionate and self-sacrificing, a man of principle, dedicated to helping others. His name suggests deliverance and redemption, values that exceed the imperatives of physical existence. Jim learns from and is aided by both men, who may be seen to embody the two conflicting, competing aspects of his being: the drive for personal, physical survival and the aspiration toward an ethical principle by which to live, toward a moral conception of life.

Jim's changing relationship to Basie and to Ransome in the course of the novel is a gauge of the state of his inner conflict. From Basie, Jim learns tactics of survival, and what is more important, absorbs from him a sort of indomitable animal optimism that prevents him from succumbing to passivity and despair or to his own death-wish. Jim's initial nursing of Basie, restoring him to health, possesses an inner correspondence with Jim's awakening to and cultivation of his own survival instincts. Basie is a source of sustenance for Jim throughout the years of captivity at Lunghua Camp, but he exacts his due in terms of obedience and obeisance. After the end of the war, Jim recognizes all too clearly the limitations of Basie: "His one strength was that he never allowed himself to dream" (254). Jim also perceives the mortal danger to himself attendant upon an alliance with Basie, and, at last, contrives to free himself from Basie's influence, luring the insatiably greedy steward to his probable death.

At the outset of their acquaintance Jim's attitude toward Dr. Ransome is one of disgust mingled with an element of fear of disapproval. Jim, who has already endured extremes of privation before meeting the doctor, considers Ransome naive. Even after many years of shared captivity and hardships, Jim continues to regard Dr. Ransome as being essentially "misguided" (147) though he privately concedes that his "only close bond in Lunghua" (161) is that which he has formed with Dr. Ransome. Throughout their relationship Dr. Ransome frequently sacrifices his own meager ration of food to supplement Jim's, doing so to the extent that during the three years at Lunghua Camp "Dr. Ransome's large body had shrunk and wasted" (153). In a metaphoric sense this may be seen to represent the diminishment of Jim's own moral sense as his instincts of survival gain ascendancy and grow apace.

Yet Jim's determination to keep Dr. Ransome alive, bartering with Basie for food for Dr. Ransome, would seem to indicate his unwillingness to forsake wholly the values that the doctor embodies or to permit them to be lost. Indeed, Jim's later care for Mr. Maxted, together with his other small acts of kindness and mercy to his fellow prisoners during the forced march from the camp to the Nantao stadium, show that Dr. Ransome's example has not been lost upon Jim, and that Jim has, in fact, internalized the doctor's values and orientation rather than those of Basie. From Dr. Ransome, Jim has learned to conjugate the verb *amo* (to love) in more than a literal sense. Significantly, too, Dr. Ransome survives the war, his ideals intact, and in the end, following the disappearance of Basie, he and Jim are re-united and reconciled.

But beyond the orientations represented by Basie and Dr. Ransome, there is a third energy, a third aspect of Jim's psyche that seeks realization: his spiritual aspirations, which express themselves in dreams of flight and through imagery of light. Jim's keen interest in model aircraft, in man-lifting kites, and in all that is associated with flight dates from before the outbreak of the war with Japan, but during his captivity his dreams of flying and his fascination with aircraft assume a peculiar, potent influence in his mind. Jim's fever-vision of silver airplanes, which he believes to be American aircraft, serves to comfort and sustain him through his many tribulations. This vision is subsequently fused with his admiration for the Japanese kamikaze pilots with their contempt for death. Both literally and symbolically Jim is saved from death by pilots: the Japanese pilots who save him from the work gang, the American pilots who drop canisters of food.

Pilots and planes take on a numinous quality in Jim's imagination. In what is a sort of private religion, Jim sees the American and Japanese aircraft as vehicles of redemption, as "pieces of the sun" (179), and the pilots as emissaries of light, as "archangelic" (155) figures. Jim's seeming resurrection of a dead Japanese pilot is the climactic event of the novel, and may be seen as emblematic of his own inner resurrection, the rebirth of his psyche that was shattered by the violence he witnessed and the isolation and insecurity he endured. The "exploding boy" (44), the "deformed figure in the fractured miror" (45) has re-integrated and reconstructed himself, and has been revived as a new, whole, and mature person.

The ultimate terms of *Empire of the Sun* are reflected in the equivocal title of the novel, which may be read as referring both to the Empire of Japan with its rising sun emblem, and to the true, transcendent empire of the sun, the realm of eternal light of which the silver airplanes seen in dreams are emissaries. Temporal power, the might and pride of nations and races, their terrible, destructive quarrels, all these exist in relation to the realm of the infinite as darkness to light, as falsehood to truth. In this manner, then, despite the persistence of the distorted images of the cinema newsreels which, at the conclusion of the novel, are seen to dominate the post-war world, imposing their own truths upon the war, perpetuating illusion and helping to ensure future conflict, there also persist in the world instants of clarity and occasions of vision: the glint and gleam of light from aircraft in flight that remind us of our true identity and our real destiny and destination, and the beckoning, momentary blankness of a movie screen from which the images have disappeared and upon which we suddenly behold "a rectangle of silver light . . . in the night air, a window into another universe" (277). Seen in this perspective, Jim's division, conflict, and metamorphosis represent an analogue to the process of cosmic evolution, the almost imperceptibly slow alchemical transmutation of the base to the precious, of the finite to the infinite, the aeon-long distillation of darkness to light.

Another step in the slow process of universal transmutation is executed, another battle in the continuing struggle between image and vision, ego and unconscious, is enacted in *The Day of Creation*.[4] Taking place in the near future, in a central African state, during a period of prolonged and severe drought in that region of the world, the novel concerns the sudden appearance, brief flourishing, and abrupt disappearance of a mighty river, the Mallory, named for the narrator of the story, Dr. Mallory, an English physician attached to the World Health Organization, who is the discoverer, or rather, as it would seem, the creator of the river.

The destinies of Dr. Mallory and of the river which is named for him are interrelated in such a manner that the two may ultimately be seen as twin aspects of a single identity. The river represents a manifestation of an unknown self, an alternative, parallel Mallory for which Dr. Mallory has unknowingly been searching much of his life. Dr. Mallory's strange hostility to the river, which he sees as his rival, his repeated attempts to destroy it, and his gradual acceptance and recognition of the true nature and significance of the river constitute the central thematic movement of the novel.

In a sense, Dr. Mallory's quest to discover and to release an unknown identity begins long before his arrival in Africa. For a period of ten years since becoming a qualified physician he has been avoiding the actual practice of medicine as much as possible, until an obscure sense of destiny brings him to a conflict-torn, drought-ravaged, famine-stricken central African republic. Here he contrives to initiate a drilling project in search of underground water with which to irrigate the dying land and to fructify the encroaching desert. Mallory's evasion of a medical career would seem to have been an unconscious stratagem to compel himself to pursue his true aim and to exercise his peculiar power, even though he is quite unaware of both of these at a conscious level. Dr. Mallory's eventual, accidental discovery or invention of a water source represents the discovery of his latent, other self, as suggested by his immediate sight of himself reflected in the water of the spring: "I gazed down, seeing my own face reflected in the black mirror" (38), and by his act of bathing himself with the waters of the newly created river, washing from himself a layer of dust and thereby "revealing a second darker skin" (44).

From the outset, Dr. Mallory's attitude toward the Mallory is one of ambivalence. He resists the river, attempting on numerous occasions to destroy it by damming, diverting, or draining it. Yet he is also irresistibly drawn by the river, proud of having created it, feeling an early sense of proprietorship with regard to it, and then a growing sense of identity with the river that bears his name.

Mallory's ambivalence toward the river is a reflection of his own self-dividedness, the conflict within his psyche between the forces of creation and those of destruction, between his desire to re-fructify and to redeem the arid land, the desert, and the world, and his desire to annihilate himself. This conflict is, in turn, reflected in his name: he is called both Doctor Mallory and Doc Mal, the former recalling the piety and high ideals of the Arthurian knights of Sir Thomas Malory's *Morte Darthur*, while the latter appellation suggests sickness and evil.

The river is a correlative image of Dr. Mallory's psyche, the course of the Mallory's waters corresponding to the inner conflict, the doubts, and aspirations of the doctor: dividing into two channels below its headwaters, the Mallory later loses itself among a maze of marshes, swamps, and lagoons, "as if trying to conceal its identity from itself" (150); the river redefines itself again into a single, clear channel, but is subsequently restrained by a dam, its diverted waters growing stagnant and poisonous, breeding pestilence. At the same time, the Mallory corresponds to stages or layers of Dr. Mallory's consciousness: its lower reaches are "the domestic realm of the small mammals . . . the passerine birds and flowering plants" (152), its middle waters changing to become "the more primitive world of the amphibians and raptors" (152), and its upper regions constituting a primordial zone "outside time or memory" (240). In this sense, Dr. Mallory's ascent of the river Mallory in search of its source represents a journey inward, a quest for the original fount of his own conscious being.

In the tradition of the Ballard hero, Dr. Mallory undergoes a process of ordeal and metamorphosis in the course of his quest. He endures injury, malnutrition, exposure, exhaustion, and fever on his journey up the Mallory, as well as being pursued, meanaced, fired upon, and captured by the various rival factions seeking to exploit the river for their own puposes, whether ideological or those of personal vengeance or ambition. Dr. Mallory is refined by his privations and sufferings to the degree that he experiences a psychic rebirth, resolving his inner division, overcoming his destructive urges and his death-wish, and becoming transformed into a new, whole man. His symbolic resurrection from below-decks of the death-ship *Diana*—"Like a talcumed corpse springing through the lid of a coffin, I burst between the bone-white planks" (226)— signals the culmination of his metamorphosis and coincides almost exactly with the breaking of the dam, freeing at last the pent and poisoned waters of the Mallory, but representing also the onset of the river's death throes.

The Mallory dies through Dr. Mallory's "failure of will," through "a sickening of the imaginative force which had created the Mallory" (186). The dam that restrains and diverts its waters has its counterpart in Mallory's psyche, and he does not succeed in breaking down the inward barrage before the dream that has created and sustained the river begins to die in his mind. Despite his desperate efforts to revive the Mallory at its source, the river dies in his arms. But Dr. Mallory has, in the course of his quest, attained sufficient wisdom and psychic strength to believe that the Mallory will return, that the mysterious power that brought it to life is neither dead nor utterly spent but only dormant once more. Beside the drained lake where the Mallory first appeared, Dr. Mallory maintains a vigil, faithful to his belief in the eventual, inevitable resurrection of the river.

Dr. Mallory's companion on his quest for the source of the river is a twelve-year-old native girl named Noon, a member of the local guerrilla force though her tribal affiliation is with a remote, primitive mountain tribe. One of Noon's earliest acts with regard to Dr. Mallory takes place during a guerrilla action when she deliberately takes aim at him and pulls the trigger of her rifle, though without the weapon discharging. Mallory later discovers that although the magazine of the rifle was loaded and locked, Noon had failed to chamber a round. The doctor is left to wonder whether the act was deliberate or a miscalculation, a gesture of contempt, a provocation, or even the enactment of a ritual death. Perhaps in some manner this mock-death precipitates the release of Dr. Mallory's dormant powers, enabling him to discover/create the river. Noon is inscrutable, but her central purpose is clear: to defend the Mallory and to goad and to guide Dr. Mallory up the river to its source. Noon undertakes to steer the boat that the doctor has stolen and navigates it around obstacles in the river as if somehow unconsciously she knows the whole course of the Mallory. It is the doctor's belief that she is secretly privy to all of his thoughts and motives as well. Noon lures and leads Mallory to the very fount of the river and then vanishes.

During the course of their journey Noon develops physically from a child to a woman. Indeed, when Mallory last glimpses her, just before her disappearance, he notes that: "her eyes were those of a woman of my own age" (250). Noon would seem to represent an anima figure, an embodiment of Mallory's deep, latent powers, a guardian spirit, a mediator between Mallory and the river, a guide to his initiation into a higher mode of consciousness. As such Noon also constitutes the key to the resurrection of the river, as Mallory recognizes: "I am waiting for a strong-shouldered young woman, with a caustic eye, walking along the drained bed of the Mallory with a familiar jaunty stride. Sooner or later she will reappear, and I am certain that when she does the Mallory will also return . . ." (254).

The phenomenon of the Mallory, its appearance and its subsequent effects, possesses mythic resonances that serve to suggest certain archetypal principles underlying the story. The most central of these is the Paradise archetype, expressed here in the Edenic transformation of the drought-stricken landscape by the Mallory: the germination of seeds long dormant, the emergence of new flora, the attraction of a myriad of birds and beasts to the lush riverine paradise of this "maiden world" (103). Dr. Mallory and Noon may be said to assume the roles of a new Adam and Eve, naked in a new Paradise, naming "new things . . . new hours and new days" (109). Appropriately, the catalyst of this new paradise is the ancient buried root-tree, a parallel to or even the remnant of the original Tree of Knowledge.

A further aspect of the Paradise archetype is manifested in the comparisons of the river to a "sleeping leviathan" (19), and to a long-dead god now revived again. These and other related images suggest the river as a metaphor for the recovery by humankind of lost power or lost grace that can lead us at last "out of the night and into the dream" (98). A corresponding archetype of the myth of Paradise is, of course, that of the Fall, which here occurs as a consequence of capitulation to egotism and to the possessiveness and impercipience and the perverse destructive urges that egotism begets: "I had become so obsessed by myself that I had seen the Mallory as a rival, and measured its currents against my own ambition. Like a child, I had wanted to destroy the river, afraid that I could not keep all of it to myself" (231).

The struggle between the river and the desert, that is between fertility and sterility, life and death, is among the most ancient, most essential archetypal dramas. The river is here characterized as the "primordial river" (55) that once fructified the now barren wastes of the Sahara, and will do so once again, overthrowing the forces of sterility and death, heralding the advent of a new Golden Age.

A final archetype associated with the river is that of the Deluge. Early in the story, Dr. Mallory is mockingly likened to Noah by the cynical and ruthlessly ambitious Captain Kagwa: "You are Noah, doctor, waiting for rain, Noah without an ark" (27). But Mallory manages to gain both water and an ark of sorts, and the Deluge eventually does occur, drowning the fighting armies of Harare and Kagwa when the dam bursts and the waters of the Mallory roll down upon them in a mighty wave.

The mythic patterns of the story serve to propose a view of experience and events as possessing a character and a purpose beyond their context in the physical world, beyond ordinary categories of explanation and interpretation. Moreover, the archetypal patterns underlying the story are also related to one of the central themes of the novel: the opposition of myth to illusion, imagination to image.

The principal agents of illusion and image in the novel are Professor Sanger and Mr. Pal, collaborators on numerous dubious television documentaries. Their precursors, Miss Matsouka and her photographer, who represent a Japanese television news network, are put out of commission relatively early in the story, and serve chiefly to introduce the motif of false, distorted perception extended and developed by Sanger and Mr. Pal. The biased selectivity demonstrated by Miss Matsouka and her photographer in their pursuit of "news" is succeeded by the far more calculated fabrications of Sanger and Pal. They view the television medium as a means to communicate "a new truth" (57) that is nothing more than a sentimentalized, sanitized, pre-digested reduction of every phenomenon, a package of comfortable illusions designed to reassure their viewers, to lull them and pacify them, and to insulate them against anything of a disturbing nature. In this manner the television medium—the image—not only serves to maintain the status quo but virtually invents it.

Sanger, with his capped teeth, his too obvious cosmetic surgery, his studied affability and bogus sincerity, all barely disguising his air of seediness, shabbiness, and decay, may be seen as the very personification of image and illusion. Myopic almost to the point of blindness, he depends for all his information about the world around him upon his counterpart, Mr. Pal, who perceives the world according to a set of rational, scientific clichés, consisting essentially of various forms of measurement, quantification, and categorization. In Sanger, Dr. Mallory recognizes a dangerous rival, more dangerous in his way than either Harare or Kagwa, for Sanger wishes not so much to exploit the phenomenon of the Mallory as to impose upon it his own image.

However, following the death of Mr. Pal, and as a result also of the extreme privations to which he is subjected, Sanger is temporarily transformed into that of which he is normally the perversion: a bardic myth-maker, a blind singer in the Homeric tradition. (It may be that Sanger's name suggests that buried identity: he embodies the past tense of a singer, as it were.) Indeed, at this point, Dr. Mallory who has reached the end of his powers of endurance, is sustained in his quest by Sanger's delirious epic visions, by his mythic imagination. Between Sanger the television documentarist and Sanger the inspired poet-seer there is a profound, irreconcilable disparity: the first distorts and reduces reality in the interest of maintaining the existing state of illusion; the second sees into reality, perceiving its essence, and seeing and communicating the higher truth beyond the realm of appearance, doing so in order to transform the phenomenal world. After the conclusion of the expedition, though, Sanger reverts completely to his former self, repudiating his mythopoetic insights, rejecting the very significance of his experience. As Dr. Mallory observes: "The irony is that, in many ways I remember our journey to the Mallory's source in terms of Sanger's imaginary travelogue. That alone seems to give meaning to all that took place" (253).

This contrast between the use of language as a means of confirming preconception, upholding the paradigms of quotidian reality, and pandering to human vanity, or as a vehicle of myth and vision, may be seen elsewhere in the novel as well. Kagwa, for example, enjoys viewing the recorded video images of himself out of sheer conceit, while hoping also that the video interview will impress his superiors and help to promote his career. Likewise, his soldiers are unable to resist the fascination of seeing themselves on the closed-circuit television screen aboard the *Diana*. Noon, however, employs Sanger's library of videos for quite another purpose, using it to discover, among the clips of 1940s Hollywood B-movie melodramas, a mythic image of herself, that of the African warrior queen. The essential difference here, as in the case of Sanger, is one of what may be called a "horizontal" use of image as opposed to a "vertical" use of image; the former merely reinforces the fixed and known, the world of "objective" fact; the latter, like a metaphor or symbol, extends consciousness into the unknown, expands the possibilities of reference and meaning, and serves as a sort of aperture through which the truths of a higher or eternal realm may be glimpsed.

The Day of Creation presents a view of the modern world as a place of fragmentation, violence, and frivolous diversion; it is a world where spirituality has been supplanted by entertainment, perception replaced by preconception, and where apotheosized technology serves the narrow ends of egotism. (Appropriately, the dam that restrains the Mallory is composed of technological artefacts.) The world of Ballard's novel is a drought-stricken wasteland whose physical dryness is the outward sign of its psychic aridity, a dying, desert world in need of revivification by the deep energies of the psyche, in need of irrigation by the fructifying energies of myth and dream. The book affirms the presence and the potency of such energies: they abide in the nether strata of our consciousness awaiting only occasions of release.

The release of long-pent energies of the unconscious in another form entirely is the subject of Ballard's most recent work at the time of this writing, a fable of apocalyptic violence, titled *Running Wild*.[5] The story is set in Pangbourne Village, an exclusive suburban housing community in contemporary England, and concerns the investigation of an appalling massacre whose victims number thirty-two men and women, or all of the adult residents of Pangbourne Village—murdered with "ruthless efficiency" (53) at the hands of their own children.

At the outset of the investigation it is believed that the Pangbourne parents were killed by terrorists, by a band of psychotics, or by foreign agents, and that their children were thereafter abducted. Indeed, the investigating authorities place the possibility of the victims having been slain by their own children at the very bottom of their list of "Bizarre Theories." Even when the evidence that the children were the sole and deliberate perpetrators of the slaughter becomes incontrovertible, both the various investigative branches and the media persist in their belief that "the young murderers were either drugged or acting under duress" (71). Such unwillingness to abandon or even to question cherished notions of reality is a recurrent theme in the novella. As the narrator, Dr. Richard Greville, one of the investigators, remarks in his forensic diaries: "My failure to recognise the obvious, in common with almost everyone else concerned, is a measure of the true mystery of the Pangbourne Massacre" (2).

The theme of illusion and delusion that is suggested by the pertinacious impercipience of the investigators and the media with regard to the Pangbourne Massacre is further sustained by the gradual discovery and disclosure of evidence concerning the true nature of the community of Pangbourne and its inhabitants. The

Pangbourne parents, as it proves, were deluded in their belief that they were serving their children's needs, satisfying their requirements and desires, and fostering their growth and development as human beings. In fact, the parents of Pangbourne were engaged in systematically—though unintentionally and unknowingly—suppressing, crushing, stunting, and starving their children, denying them the most essential requisites for human identity: love and freedom. The subtle program of behavior modification to which the children of Pangbourne were continuously subjected, the inculcation of "liberal and humane values" (10) by means of various forms of surveillance and of positive reinforcement, constituted, in actual fact, an insidious and fearfully effective mode of brainwashing, representing in the minds of the children an attempt to overwhelm and to annihilate the very foundations of individual conscience and consciousness.

According, Pangbourne Village itself, envisaged by its creators, Camelot Holdings Ltd., and by its adult occupants as a sort of earthly paradise, a small-scale utopia, a bulwark of and a nursery for enlightened, civilized values—"The New Samoa," as the proposed television documentary on Pangbourne was to have characterized the community—was in actuality a prison, an affectless, unnatural realm, insular, sterile, "eventless" (41) and severed from all sources of vitality and meaning.

The terrible and sudden eruption of violence at Pangbourne did not occur without certain warning signs and portents, but these either went unnoticed or were ignored by the parents of Pangbourne Village, blissfully impervious in their paradise of preconceptions. One such omen was the keen interest taken by the children of Pangbourne in certain sports activities whose common denominator was "the element of escape, as if the children were unconsciously equipping themselves with the means to break free from their lives" (45). This phase was succeeded by a period of complete withdrawal on the part of the children from all outdoor activities and extra-Pangbourne contacts, a retreat into their own homes and their own rooms. It is apparently from this period that the curious notches or marks found in all of the houses date, together with the secret diaries and the systematic mutilation of the volume of Piaget by Jeremy Maxted. The final and most chilling of the portents of profound malaise and imminent violence was the parody documentary film of Pangbourne which the children produced, their final version interspersing atrocity footage with scenes of idyllic, placid life at Pangbourne Village. It is known that the Maxteds, both psychiatrists, possessed a copy of this final version of the children's film. The tragedy might well have been averted if this pair of "fashionable psychiatrists" (48) had known how to read and to respond to this symbolic gesture. In common, though, with the other Pangbourne parents, the Maxteds persisted in their delusion, ruthlessly attempting to force their children to conform to an illusory prototype of the happy, well-adjusted child, rather than considering their real needs and their individual identities.

The Pangbourne parents disregard not only external signs and symptoms concerning the false paradise in which they dwell, but apparently neglect to heed internal warnings as well, if we may take the dream recorded by Charles Ogilvy as representative. Ogilvy dreams "of sailing down the Nile, a journey he and his wife made three years earlier, but in his dream the great temples and pyramids have been replaced by film sets" (62). Clearly, the dream indicates the supplanting of the authentic by the spurious, a parallel to the process which has taken place in the lives of all the Pangbourne parents. In effect, all of the Pangbourne adults live in a film set of their own design, sustaining a collective illusion that ultimately proves to be fatal for them.

In the context of this mesh of illusion and delusion, the Pangbourne Massacre may be seen to represent a desperate act of psychic self-defense, a revolt against mendacity and intolerable oppression. The notches or markings found by the investigators around the skirting boards and interior panels of doors in the houses in Pangbourne Village seemed to Dr. Greville to resemble those which might be made by "a small creature . . . trying to get out" (25). Metaphorically, that is precisely what they represent: the gnawing of the human spirit against the walls that confine and crush it, against the prison wherein it is stunted and starved.

Significantly, in this regard, the hand gestures that are endlessly repeated by the traumatized Marion Miller, gestures which are revealed ultimately to be a reenactment of her act of murder, are, at the same time, "exactly the sequence of wrist movements, according to the experts, that would release a spring-loaded mortice lock" (32). Thus, the murders represent an act of release, of escape, an assertion of liberty against tyranny, and of life against death.

Running Wild seems to suggest that the motive power of the violent revolt of the spirit that takes place at Pangbourne Village lies in the unconscious, that the terrible destructive force that drives the children to kill their own fathers and mothers is akin to or allied with the same energy that expresses itself creatively through myth, legend, and the literary imagination. Allusions in the text to the myth of the House of Atreus, to the legend of Robin Hood, to the story of Peter Pan, and to George Orwell's fable *Animal Farm* serve to indicate a context in which the Pangbourne killings may be seen to belong and in which, accordingly, they may be understood: sanctified homicide, moral outlawry, resolute resistance to the imperatives of the fallen, adult world, the revolt of natural innocence against oppression by agents of corrupt civilization. At the same time, the allusions identify the murders at Pangbourne with that attribute of the human mind which is in perpetual revolt against the tyranny of the material, temporal world: the imagination. In this sense, the ultimate terms of the story are those of the forces of reason, as exemplified by the absolute order and the sterile sanity of Pangbourne Village, in opposition to the unconscious: the redemptive powers latent in the human psyche which may manifest themselves in either a creative or a destructive manner, as circumstances compel or permit.

Running Wild is a cautionary tale, closely related to the author's novels and stories of cataclysm in that it proposes that the civilized world we have created and which we continue so devotedly to refine and to improve—the world of security and order, convenience and amusement we have made in the image of the desires of our ego-consciousness and according to the requirements of our rational intellect—is a world that thwarts our deepest needs and violates our true being. The story further suggests that if we persist in disdaining and denying our true identity, then ultimately it will exact a terrible vengeance.

Ballard's later novels develop and clarify certain essential themes of his fiction: the struggle between modes of perception and between planes of existence. These later works warn us of the consequences of perceiving the world according to formulae and fixed images, and affirm, instead, the visionary faculties of the mind, the inner eye of the mythopoeic imagination. Likewise, these books compel our attention to the ways in which we have made of our lives a prison, and of our world a desert; urging us, at the same time, to cultivate the regenerating, liberating energies of the unconscious, inciting us to free ourselves from the prisons of illusion in which we are self-incarcerated, and to strive toward the transformation of the arid wasteland of our epoch into a new, fecund Eden. They further exhort us to integrate our fragmented selves, recover our psychic equilibrium, discover our true identity, and then to embark upon "a journey to the sun," to enter upon the ultimate adventure of the self: the quest for absolute being.

Conclusion

J. G. Ballard's oeuvre possesses a remarkable inner consistency, while at the same time exhibiting very considerable variety among its constituent parts. In the foregoing discussion of Ballard's novels and short fiction I have, of course, emphasized the continuity of theme and imagery among the author's works, but I do not wish to convey the impression that they are to be considered in any sense repetitious or predictable. To the contrary, the reader is continually delighted by their range, their diversity, and their ingenuity, as well as by their aesthetic refinement. In my view, the recurrence of particular images and themes only serves to enhance the imaginative power of Ballard's fiction and to reinforce its artistic unity as a body of work.

The central theme of Ballard's fiction, configured in so many different ways and considered from such varied perspectives throughout his work, is that of a crisis of being and of consciousness, an ontological disorder which obtains at three mutually reflective levels: the cosmic, the social, and the individual.

At the first level, the temporal, material universe is seen as constituting a rupture or schism from the universe of infinite and absolute being, and is thus in itself without ultimate ontological validity: an illusion. At the second level—the social—the crisis is reflected in the entrenchment of fraud and falsehood in our society and in our daily lives in the world. The manipulations of reality perpetrated by government, by advertising and the media, together with the distorting codes and conventions of cultural conditioning, limit and misshape our perception to the degree that we may justifiably be said to dwell in a world of illusion. The primary misapprehension, from which the other two levels of illusion may be seen to proceed, is that of ego-consciousness, which consists of the error of identifying a very small part of the total psyche—the conscious personality—with the whole of the self. In this sense our very identity is an illusion.

We live, then, as fallen beings in a fallen universe, but our plight is not seen as hopeless by the author, for there persist within our psyches powerful energies that seek deliverance from the prisons-within-prisons of illusion. These energies express themselves through destruction and disaster, through myth and dream, and through desire and love. Resistance, on the part of ego-mind and society and by the nature of the phenomenological universe itself, against these psychic forces and their manifestations is as intense as it is unrelenting, but ultimately these redemptive energies are irrepressible and irresistible. They can be neither contained nor restrained indefinitely; they will slowly undermine and suddenly overthrow all checks and impediments, and, in the end, re-establish the condition of primordial unity.

Accordingly, a radical dualism at the heart of Ballard's art is expressed in the double impulse of his fiction, which represents an arraignment of the finite, as it embodies, at the same time, the quest for an ontological Eden. Ballard's work indicts all that is inimical to the evolution of consciousness, including all forms of vanity, selfishness, complacency, control, oppression, dehumanization, and the desacralization of life; while correspondingly the author's work upholds all that promotes liberty and the imagination, communion, and the growth and unfolding of the spirit.

The development of Ballard's fiction may be seen to reside in its increasingly clear focus upon the nature and character of the human predicament in its myriad modes and forms, together with the author's sustained and increasingly subtle exploration of possible solutions to the problems of identity and reality, both in their essence and in their various extensions. This development is accompanied by a clear evolution of the author's treatment of the theme of transcendence. In the earliest works the quest for an ontological Eden is portrayed as an individual undertaking, sometimes attempted in direct opposition to and in conflict with other individuals; in the later works transcendence has become a collective human endeavor undertaken in a spirit of mutuality and love. In the early fictions Ballard's apocalypses are violent and tragic; in the later works they become, for the most part, more affirmative and agreeable, even joyous and ecstatic, in character. The apocalypses also become at once more subtle and more extreme. No longer involving cataclysms, catastrophes, and disasters, they are more spiritual in character and thus more readily apprehensible as the manifestation of the will of our collective unconscious and as the fulfillment of our highest and purest desires.

The imagery by which the deepest meaning of Ballard's fiction is communicated undergoes a similar refinement, achieving a more potent compression, becoming more resonant and more pronouncedly archetypal. At the same time, the metaphysic implicit in Ballard's fictions becomes increasingly explicit and attains greater coherence. Likewise, the several themes of the author's novels and stories become more apparently elements of a central pattern of meaning, the expression of a consistent and compelling view of the world.

Given the unity of imagery and the integrity of theme in Ballard's oeuvre, his writing cannot easily be separated into major and minor works. In a sense his writing is all of a piece and it may, I believe, most profitably be considered as such. The novels and the short stories that make up his work are all mutually reflective, interrelated in such a manner that they reinforce one another's meanings and form a coherent whole. As Judith Merril has observed: "The author [Ballard] is building from book to book, and from story to story, in such a way that although each unit is meaningful on its own terms, it assumes full dimensions only in the context of the whole body of work."[1] Nevertheless, and in full recognition that inevitably there will be argument concerning my choices, I would like to indicate those novels and short stories which in my estimation represent the author's most substantial and significant works, first explaining the criteria for my selection.

The qualities that I most admire in Ballard's writing include its technical accomplishment, its imaginative power and dramatic intensity, its metaphorical suggestiveness, its mythic overtones, and the author's ability to create mood and evoke atmosphere. In addition, I particularly admire the author's skill in the portrayal of inner landscapes, his rendering of terrains and territories that are objectifications of states of spirit.

Such inner landscapes are the most primary, most vital element in Ballard's art, assuming the position ordinarily occupied by character in fiction. Indeed, it may be said that ultimately these inner landscapes are the real protagonists in Ballard's work, in the sense that they represent the true identity of the characters who interact with them and who, in the end, surrender to them, unite with them.

Accordingly, the individual works of Ballard that seem to me to be the most distinctive, the most impressive, and most effective are most frequently those in which inner landscape is a central element, though this is not my exclusive standard of judgment. The archaeopsychic landscape of *The Drowned World*; the visionary, jewelled landscape of the crystallized forest in *The Crystal World*; the neglected, sentient landscape of weeds and ruins in *Concrete Island*; and the lush, paradisiac jungle that springs suddenly from a drought-stricken wasteland in *The Day of Creation*—these represent for me Ballard's highest achievements in the novel form. In these books the author renders meticulously imagined worlds, vivid, compelling, alive with detail, and possessing profound psychic resonances. Among the author's short fiction the most intensely visualized inner landscapes include those depicted in "The Voices of Time," "A Question of Re-entry," "The Terminal Beach," "Myths of the Near Future," together with several of the short prose pieces that make up *The Atrocity Exhibition*. The drained swimming pools and deserts, the fertile jungles and rusting gantries, the abandoned concrete bunkers and weapons ranges, the deserted car parks and flyovers of these stories constitute the essential vocabulary of Ballard's art.

An additional reason for my selection of the above-named novels and stories as representing the author's most successful and satisfying works is that I also regard them as the quintessential presentations of another significant feature of the author's work, namely the delineation of the Ballardian hero. The protagonists of Ballard's novels and stories, in spite of differing surface characteristics and circumstances, tend to possess certain common qualities that together comprise a distinctive type of hero that is a hallmark of Ballard's fiction.

Although the protagonists of the author's works are most often middle-aged, middle-class professionals (frequently medical doctors), they are invariably self-divided men, alienated, introspective, motivated by impulses mysterious to them. They may be described as mystics-in-spite-of-themselves—witty, urbane individuals who find themselves somehow compelled to pursue self-liberation and to enter upon a quest for the absolute. Usually these figures manage for a time to maintain a certain wry attitude and ironic distance to the unexpected, incomprehensible expression of their inner, other identity, but in the end they achieve the courage of their compulsions and find fulfillment in surrender to the forces of the unconscious. This type of protagonist—as stylized in its way as the "code hero" of Ernest Hemingway's fiction—seems particularly appropriate to the post-war and post-modern West, serving to document the contemporary crisis of identity, to represent the ennui, the anomie, the restlessness of modern technological man, in whom, despite material well-being and sophisticated, socially-sanctioned hedonism, the appetite for the infinite irrepressibly expresses itself.

There are, in addition to the works I have indicated above, a number of excellent short storiers, equal in distinction to those I have already named, which are not centered upon imagery of inner landscape. Their strength derives, instead, from their allegorical power. These include "Minus One," "The Drowned Giant," "End Game," "My Dream of Flying to Wake Island," "Motel Architecture," and "War Fever." The particular merit of these stories resides in their concise, incisive penetration of vital human issues, and in the author's assured and expert control of his medium. In common with the inner-landscape novels and stories, these stories seem to me to represent at its most intense and most effective the power of Ballard's fiction to engage, to intrigue, to disturb, and to enlarge us.

J. G. Ballard's mythical, mystical fiction represents something of an anomaly amid the literary currents of post-war and contemporary England. In the first place, Ballard comes from the outside, from the literary "ghetto" of science fiction with its pulps and paperbacks, an author who has built a readership beyond the boundaries of the usual literary audience, who has established a reputation independent of the customary literary apparatus. Moreover, and perhaps more to the point, Ballard's work does not share either the realist mode or the socio-moral preoccupations of the mainstream English novel, nor, on the other hand, does it possess any real affinities with the self-conscious, self-parodying meta-fictional codes characteristic of the anti-novel. Neither properly "of the tradition" as it is currently defined, nor yet truly avant-garde in character, Ballard's fiction thus falls outside of the various fashions and fads, such as "angry," existentialist, post-modern, post-structuralist, neo-formalist, and so on, which have succeeded each other with such rapidity (and vapidity) during the decades since the end of the war, that is, during the period in which Ballard has written and published his work.

At the same time, however, it should be noted that aspects of Ballard's work resonate with elements in the writing of certain authors of the post-war era. Samuel Beckett's landscapes of desolation and disintegration find an echo in the motif of aridity, decay, and dereliction so prominent in Ballard's fiction. George Orwell's dystopian terrors and his awareness of the dangerous manipulative potentials of language and of the media are likewise reflected in Ballard's writing, as is also something of the tortured spirituality that animates the novels of Graham Greene and William Golding. (There seem to be echoes of Greene's *A Burnt Out Case* in *The*

Crystal World, and echoes, perhaps, of Golding's *Pincher Martin* in *Concrete Island*.) Lawrence Durrell's sense of the liberating power of sexuality and his attempts to evolve a secular metaphysics can be said to have certain affinities with Ballard's themes of the powers of the unconscious and the urge for transcendence. In the same manner, the Manicheanism central to Anthony Burgess's fiction possesses significant similarities with the radical dualism that informs Ballard's writing. In this sense, Ballard's fiction may be seen to be allied in certain ways with that of other British writers of the period in its confrontation with a fragmented, enervated world in which orthodox religious perspectives and traditional humanist notions of culture and progress alike have collapsed, and in its collision with a fictive reality that is the invention of technology, advertising, public relations, and the communications media.

Among his American contemporaries, Ballard may be said to share a certain amount of common ground with Philip K. Dick, and a good more than that with William S. Burroughs. The affinities that exist between Ballard's writing and the writing of Philip K. Dick are essentially those of genre and theme. Both authors have approached the science-fiction medium in a highly personal, idiosyncratic manner, adapting the medium to their vision, and creating within the field of s-f vital and distinctive bodies of work that have successfully challenged certain of the conventions of the genre and have served to extend its perimeters and expand its parameters. Both authors are concerned in their work with issues of identity and perception and with metaphysical questions. The writings of Ballard and of Dick may alike be characterized as being explorations of inner psychic universes, inquiries into the nature of consciousness and cognition, into reality and illusion, into solipsism and transcendence. Similarly, as a concomitant theme, both writers also deal with the complicity of the media, government, and commercial interests in fabricating a false, fraudulent reality.

Closer and more numerous affinities may be seen between Ballard's work and that of William S. Burroughs. Science fiction has exerted considerable influence upon Burroughs' writing, and his novels have, in turn, exerted a marked influence upon the science-fiction medium. A mutual artistic respect and admiration exists between Ballard and Burroughs; not only has Ballard repeatedly expressed approbation with regard to Burroughs' work, but Burroughs has returned the compliment by writing a preface to the American edition of *The Atrocity Exhibition*.[2] The fictions of Ballard and of Burroughs share a number of significant characteristics, including certain common themes and motifs, together with particular parallels of style and tone.

The theme of the quest is prominent in the writing of both authors. In Ballard's fiction, as we have seen, the goal of the quest is that of discovering or repossessing an ontological Eden. Similarly, the protagonists of Burroughs' fiction are in search of inner freedom, freedom of being, freedom from the limitations of physical existence and being-in-time. In the writing of both authors this quest is often pursued against the background of corrupt, venal, disintegrating, or authoritarian societies; and for both authors the end of the quest is the achievement of true being and identity through the liberation of consciousness from the realm of time and matter.

A concomitant theme to the theme of the quest for transcendence in the work of both Ballard and Burroughs is that of liberation from the controlling mechanisms of cultural conditioning and language, and from the manipulation to which the mind is subject through the images created by the mass media, by advertising and government. Both authors regard as pernicious the formulae and clichés disseminated through photojournalism, film, television, and other media. Of equal detriment to the human spirit, in their view, are the inherited, unquestioned habits of perception and conception according to which we apprehend the world. Ballard and Burroughs concur that our notions of the world and of reality are spurious, that they are frauds perpetrated by vested interests and perpetuated by our reductive and stereotyped thinking. To oppose the illusions and delusions by which we are imprisoned and oppressed, both authors propose alternative modes of perception, including those of dream and vision, and alternative modes of conceptualization, those of intuitive cognition and of metaphoric or mythic thought. Ballard and Burroughs would also seem to be in agreement that the power structures which manipulate human consciousness and the agencies which enforce spiritual inertia and staticity may ultimately provoke extreme means of resistance from the forces which they inhibit and restrain. Such extreme means may include the sort of insurrection of the young depicted in Burroughs' *The Wild Boys* (1971), and in Ballard's *Running Wild*, and may extend also to disaster and apocalypse, themes prominent in Ballard's work, and recurrent also in Burroughs' writing, as for example in the "Gongs of Violence" section of *The Soft Machine* (1961), the "So Pack Your Ermines" section of *Nova Express* (1964), and in the "Wind Die. You Die. We Die" section of *Exterminator* (1974).

Ballard and Burroughs also share in their works a vision of sexuality as a subversive power, an expression of the energy of the unconscious that can serve to counter the forces of confinement and control. For Burroughs it is the Orgone theory of Wilhelm Reich that serves as an inspiration for the depiction of sexuality in his fiction, while the particular erotovisionary views implicit in Ballard's work would seem to derive from the writings of William Blake and perhaps also from the surrealist tradition in which the liberating power of the erotic is affirmed. In the writings of both authors, sexuality is seen to represent a regenerative power which—through its ability to overwhelm the will of the conscious self and even to suspend its existence—promotes destabilization of the ego. By virtue of its capacity for resisting subjugation sexuality serves to effect disruption of oppressive social order. It is seen as a primal, protean force furthering transgression and transcendence.

Further correspondences exist between the work of Ballard and Burroughs in the extensive and similar treatment by both authors in their fiction of the theme of dystopia. The dystopian theme is prominent throughout Burroughs' writing, from the "Interzone" of *Naked Lunch* (1959) to *Cities of the Red Night* (1981); in Ballard's fiction its range extends from the diverse types of future totalitarian societies depicted in stories such as "Build-up," "Chronopolis,"

"Passport to Eternity," and "Billenium" to the subtler but no less oppressive near-contemporary dystopias such as those presented in "The Subliminal Man" and in *Running Wild*. In the work of both authors the dystopian theme serves as a critique of incipient totalitarianism in our present culture and society, including especially the potential for dehumanization inherent in certain current forms of social engineering and in the increasing dominance of communications technology, as well as in advertising, political propaganda, consumerism, and other such forces that impend upon individual liberty and metaphysical values.

Some final affinities between the work of Ballard and Burroughs are those of technique: corresponding patterns of imagery in the writing of the two authors, together with certain similarities of style and tone. Both writers employ in their fiction imagery which may be termed that of the waste land. Recurrent motifs in their works include scenes of desolation and decay, blighted landscapes, arid zones, endless, enervated megapolises or abandoned cities, ruins and wreckage, encroaching jungles or deserts, stagnant swamps, and lagoons, all pervaded by a sense of inertia and malaise. In the work of both authors such images serve to convey a sense of the inner ruin and the spiritual devastation of contemporary humankind, and thus support the authors' central themes of the quest for transcendence and the necessity for resistance to the forces and agencies of psychic entropy.

In terms of style and tone, both authors—each in his own manner—use precise, neutral language in describing even the most hallucinated and grotesque scenes. (This stylistic affinity may derive from the early medical training of both writers.) In this manner the authors propose to counteract the corruption of language on the part of commercial and ideological interests, together with government and the media. At times also both Ballard and Burroughs employ devices of narrative fragmentation and syntactical dislocation which have the effect of liberating the reader from the temporal and physical dimensions implicit in language. Ballard uses these devices extensively only in *The Atrocity Exhibition* and in a few short stories; Burroughs employs such techniques throughout his work. In addition, both writers in their fiction effectively utilize elements of irony, satire, and black humor as weapons to resist, to expose, and to undermine those verbal and perceptual structures and those conditioning forces that working together impose and maintain a pseudo-reality that constricts consciousness and impedes psychic evolution.

Although both Ballard and Burroughs may be said to draw upon similar imaginative resources—those of dream and myth, the world of the unconscious—each writer clearly possesses a distinctive voice and vision, and each has created an imaginative territory that is uniquely and unmistakably his own. Of the two writers, Burroughs is the more innovative, the more daring in terms of content and the more radical in terms of style. Burroughs is also a more savage satirist than Ballard, and may be said to be altogether more extreme and more obsessive in his approach to fiction. Ballard, on the other hand, possesses the greater range as a writer, his oeuvre is more diverse, richer, and more complex than that of Burroughs, and his vision as an artist is more inclusive and more affirmative. Ballard's satire is tempered with a wry and subtle humor, and the characters in his fictions are far more fully realized than the anonymous narrators and grotesques that people the works of Burroughs. Moreover, Ballard is capable of depicting in his fiction ontological Edens that possess a mythic, visionary, numinous quality that is quite different from (and in my estimation far more appealing and satisfying than) the utopias of Burroughs' writing, such as the savage tribal-occult utopia of *The Wild Boys* or the techno-libertarian communes in *Cities of the Red Night*. Fortunately, of course, we need not choose between Ballard and Burroughs. We can read both writers, both of whose works provide valuable insights into the character of contemporary culture and the nature of human consciousness. The parallels and points of contact that exist between the writing of America's "literary outlaw" and Britain's literary maverick are such that they serve to illuminate and to clarify the vision of both authors.

Ballard's work occupies a special position within the field of science fiction where his writing has exerted a catalytic influence upon the genre. Ballard may be seen as one of the prophets of and a central figure in the New Wave movement in science fiction which began in England in the mid-1960s. The New Wave movement, centered on *New Worlds* magazine during the period of its editorship by Michael Moorcock, represented an attempt on the part of those authors associated with the phenomenon to revitalize the writing of science fiction by liberating the genre from the ideological and artistic restrictions imposed upon it by editors either for commercial reasons or as a reflection of their own idiosyncratic and intransigent views of what was permissible and desirable in the medium. The New Wave writers wished to exploit the potential they perceived in science fiction as a vehicle for serious literary experimentation and as a medium for more pointed social commentary. They viewed certain of the established formulae of the science-fiction genre as being hopelessly trite and the narrative techniques as unduly primitive and simplistic. They responded by introducing unorthodox subjects together with new devices of and fresh approaches to narration, extending both the thematic and the stylistic range of the medium.

Much of the New Wave challenge to the traditional idioms of science fiction was prefigured already in a guest editorial by Ballard entitled "Which Way to Inner Space?" It appeared in the May 1962 number of *New Worlds* (then under the editorship of John Carnell.)[3] In his editorial, a kind of aesthetic manifesto and an artistic credo, Ballard diagnoses a general lassitude in the field of science fiction, a loss of vitality and direction among writers, and an incipient boredom on the part of the readers. Ballard sees the cause of the condition as being twofold in nature: specifically, it is the result of the "narrow imaginative limits" inherent in "the rocket and planet story" (3); more generally, it is caused by the marked tendency among science-fiction writers merely to reshuffle hackneyed plots and themes rather than to attempt to discover new sources of inspiration and vision. Ballard warns that unless the medium summons the will and finds the means to renew itself radically it will decline into triviality and inconsequentiality.

In order to avoid such an end, and in order to maintain science fiction's role as "imaginative interpreter of the future" (116), Ballard urges writers and readers to consider a series of alterations designed to correct and improve the science-fiction medium:

> Firstly, I think science fiction should turn its back on space, on interstellar travel, extraterrestrial life forms, galactic wars and the overlap of these ideas that spreads across the margins of nine-tenths of magazine s-f. . . . Similarly, I think science fiction must jettison its present narrative forms and plots. Most of these are far too explicit to express any subtle interplay of character and theme. Devices such as time travel and telepathy, for example, save the writer the trouble of describing the inter-relationships of time and space indirectly. And by a curious paradox they prevent him from using his imagination at all, giving him very little true freedom of movement within the narrow limits set by the device.
>
> The biggest developments of the immediate future will take place, not on the Moon or Mars, but on Earth, and it is *inner* space, not outer, that needs to be explored. The only truly alien planet is Earth. . . .
>
> More precisely, I'd like to see s-f becoming abstract and 'cool,' inventing completely fresh situations and contexts that illustrate its theme obliquely. For example, instead of treating time like a sort of glorified scenic railway, I'd like to see it used for what it is, one of the perspectives of the personality, and the elaboration of concepts such as the time zone, deep time, and archaeopsychic time. I'd like to see more psycholiterary ideas, more meta-biological and metachemical concepts, private time-systems, synthetic psychologies and space-times, more of the remote, sombre half-worlds one glimpses in the paintings of schizophrenics, all in all a complete speculative poetry and fantasy of science. (117–118)

In keeping with his call for a thematic and stylistic reinvigoration of science fiction, Ballard has since consistently eschewed the commonplace props of the s-f storehouse—rockets, robots, mutants, androids, psionics, teleportation, interplanetary and interstellar travel, encounters with aliens, invasions from space, etc.— developing instead a new repertoire of motifs concerned with problems of cultural evolution and of human psychology and spirituality in relation to social and technological change. At the same time, the author has cultivated new modes of expression and explored the use of new stylistic devices and narrative techniques, employing syntactic dislocation, fragmentation, and juxtaposition to create verbal collages, eliminating sequential narrative, writing with extreme compression, combining the detachment and precision of a textbook or a scientific report with the hallucinatory inconsequence of a dream, integrating terminology drawn from the medical and psychiatric fields with lyrical passages abounding in metaphors and similes, uniting by these and other means the outer world of objects and phenomena with the inner world of the psyche, the universe of "inner space."

Although Ballard's experimentation has provoked considerable controversy and has evoked negative responses from adherents of the mainstream and the "Old Guard" of s-f, Ballard has, I believe, succeeded both in generating a new idiom of consciousness within the science-fiction field and in infusing the medium with a new sense of artistic possibility. And, in following his own recommendations with regard to new themes and treatments, he has also achieved the creation of a vital and original body of work informed by a distinctive vision and characterized by invention, innovation, and individual voice.

The anomalousness of Ballard's work mentioned earlier, its somewhat uneasy and ambiguous relation to the central trends of postwar British fiction, may also be seen in its relation to the science-fiction medium from whose norms and conventions the author has also deviated to a marked degree. Ballard is, then, something in the nature of a maverick author, the character of whose art resists strict categorization. Nevertheless, Ballard's fiction possesses significant affinities with the prose romance and with certain of the essential tenets of the English Romantic tradition.

The prose romance, whose ancestors include myth, folklore, ancient epic, and medieval chivalric romance, represents an alternative fictional mode to that of the novel proper, a counter-tradition within the history of the English novel. Unencumbered by the conventions and restrictions of realism, the prose romance cultivates the power of the imagination in its most heightened mode, while, correspondingly, its concerns are not the commonplace themes of the familiar world, but the terrors and wonders of the human mind. In its chief manifestation as the Gothic novel, during the period of the late eighteenth and early nineteenth centuries, the prose romance reintroduced to literature the dark realm of the irrational, the world of the unconscious, traditionally neglected or slighted by the novel proper.

That Ballard's fiction is heir to the spirit of the prose romance may be seen in the several characteristics they share: the journey of discovery and the quest for the ultimate as recurrent motifs; the prominence of the theme of human duality; the exploration of buried desires, of compulsions, and perverse impulses; the working out of psychological patterns in symbolic form; the affinity with dreams; the metaphysical resonances of an imagery that is disturbing and exalting in its effects; the use of simplified characters and of solitary, self-divided protagonists; the employment of exotic settings and of extreme situations; the fevered and frantic atmosphere; and the cultivation of the bizarre, the wondrous, and the fantastic. Above all, though, Ballard's work shares with the prose romance the quality of being impelled by the power of the unconscious and of being inbued with its energies.

Ballard's work also evinces kinship with central elements of the English Romantic tradition. Some general attributes common to Ballard's art and to that of the Romantics include: a preoccupation with the infinite and the transcendental; a sense of the spiritual correspondence that exists between humankind and the natural world; an intense concern with perception and the nature of reality; and a recognition that the visionary imagination represents a link with the realm of the eternal. Likewise, Ballard's work shares with the spirit of English Romanticism a fundamental distrust of scientific and technological progress, of existing social and political institutions, as well as commercial interests; and an enmity toward all forces and agencies that seek to control and to manipulate, and toward all that perpetuates custom, convention, and habit, that limits and distorts perception, and that causes oppression or sustains illusion in any form or at any level.

More specifically—to cite a few representative instances—parallels may be seen between motifs in Ballard's writing and in

the writing of William Blake, William Wordsworth, Samuel Taylor
Coleridge, Percy Bysshe Shelley, and Emily Brontë, as well as in
the paintings of John Martin. Ballard's work shares with that of
Blake not only an essentially mystical and mythopoeic character,
but also the notion that sexuality and spirituality are complementary modes of attaining to higher reality, or as Blake states: "the
whole creation will be consumed, and appear infinite and holy,
whereas it now appears finite & corrupt. This will come to pass by
an improvement of sensual enjoyment" (*The Marriage of Heaven
and Hell*, Plate 14). Ballard expresses his vision of a similar
sexo-spiritual apocalypse in such stories as "News from the Sun"
and "Myths of the Near Future," developing the theme most fully
in *The Unlimited Dream Company*, whose savior-protagonist is
named Blake.

Ballard further suggests in the story "News from the Sun" that
"The babbling new-born were telling their mothers of the realm of
wonder from which they had just been expelled" (News, 111).
Clearly, there is an echo here of Wordsworth's poetic postulate in
his famous "Ode: Intimations of Immortality from Recollections
of Early Childhood" concerning a state of pre-existence characterized by visionary splendor, a state of being from which our
earthly life is an exile, but which as infants we can still vividly
recall. In a similar manner, the numerous allusions and parallels in
Ballard's work to Coleridge's "The Rime of the Ancient Mariner"
serve to point up thematic affinities between the two writers,
especially regarding the invisible powers of the world and the
penalties attendant upon our violation of or disregard for these
powers.

There are obvious affinites between the Neo-Platonism of Shelley and certain of the concepts that inform Ballard's writing, and
there are further points of contact between Shelley's myth of
apocalypse and universal regeneration expressed in *Prometheus
Unbound* and Ballard's catastrophes and Edenic visions. An in-
cidental kinship may be seen in the employment by both writers
of imagery of night and of the sun, of sleeping and of waking, and
of flight and of ascendance, as metaphors for material existence and

for absolute being, for ego-consciousness and transcendent consciousness, and for the process or act of transcendence, respectively. Ballard may also be seen to share aspects of Emily Brontë's vision of the divided human psyche and of the overwhelming compulsions that drive us toward ecstatic self-annihilation. The transformations undergone by the characters of Catherine and Heathcliff in *Wuthering Heights*, their neglect of their physical needs, their wasted bodies and fevered minds, as they seek to release themselves from the material world and enter another dimension of being, might serve as prototypes for Ballard's obsessed protagonists who undergo similar torments and transfigurations, and who strive to attain the same goal.

An intriguing kinship also exists between Ballard's tales of disaster and the cataclysmic, apocalyptic paintings of the English Romantic artist, John Martin (1789–1854). Recurrent motifs in Martin's painting are those of catastrophic natural upheaval and of the destructive force of divine retribution—themes which, in altered form, are central to Ballard's writing. Martin's art is imbued with a sense of the infinite, and his vast, visionary canvases include: *The Deluge*, *The Fall of Babylon*, *The Fall of Nineveh*, *The Destruction of Herculaneum and Pompeii*, *The Last Judgement*, and *The Great Day of His Wrath*. In a different mood altogether from that of these turbulent, terrifying renderings of stricken cities and perishing civilizations are Martin's tranquil, ethereal depictions of *The Garden of Eden* and *The Plains of Heaven*. These motifs, once again in altered form, are vital elements also in the work of Ballard. Separated by a century and expressing themselves in different artistic media, John Martin and J. G. Ballard are nevertheless united in a common arraignment of the finite and in a shared quest for an ontological paradise.

The above-named literary movements, together with the various writers and the one painter, are mentioned here with the intention of proposing certain precursors and ancestors of Ballard's art. They are not referred to with the purpose of indicating influence or of implying derivation or imitation, but rather with that of suggesting a cultural context, a tradition in terms of which Ballard's writing may be considered. A more direct source of inspiration for Ballard's fiction is pictorial surrealism, the oneiric world of enigma, menace, eroticism, violence, beauty, terror, and revelation as it is depicted in the paintings of Max Ernst, Yves Tanguy, Salvador Dali, Oscar Dominguez, Paul Delvaux, René Magritte, and Giorgio de Chirico—the latter a proto-surrealist or "metaphysical" painter.

Allusions to the foregoing artists are frequent in Ballard's writing, and particular paintings by the above-mentioned artists sometimes provide points of reference or prophetic images in his fictions, as do, for example, Tanguy's "Jours de Lenteur" in *The Drought*, and Delvaux's "The Echo" in "The Day of Forever," to name just two such instances. More specifically, there are affinities of atmosphere and of imagery between Ballard's fiction and visual surrealism. Ernst's paintings with their silent forests and primeval swamps, their post-apocalyptic ruins and eroded rocks; the ominous and nostalgic stillness of de Chirico's deserted and shadowed cityscapes; Dali's obsessions with time and entropy; Tanguy's prehistoric or post-historic beaches suggestive of a realm beyond time and causality; the oneiric terrains and psychic geologies of Dominguez's decalcomania canvases have all evoked responses from Ballard that are reflected in the images of terminal beaches and desolate concrete carparks, empty arid zones and lush lagoons, drained swimming pools and drowned cities, dunes and ruins and jewelled jungles, that distinguish his fiction. Like those of the surrealists, Ballard's landscapes are mindscapes, externalizations of inner, psychic states, possessing precisely that quality which the author has ascribed to the imagery of pictorial surrealism, the attribute of representing an "iconography of inner space."[4]

Similarly, the juxtapositions and metamorphoses characteristic of surrealist painting are also discernible in Ballard's predilection for wild incongruities and for extremes of physical and psychic transformation. Images such as the marching Presidents of the United States in *Hello America*, the cannibalistic tribes of urban professionals in *High Rise*, or the mechanized sexual acts of *Crash* represent verbal equivalents to some of the effects achieved in surrealist art, and the metamorphoses imposed upon landscapes or undergone by individual characters in various of the author's stories and novels or by an entire town in *The Unlimited Dream Company* may be seen to correspond to those transformations rendered on canvas by the surrealist painters. A final affinity between surrealist art and the fiction of J. G. Ballard consists in their common fascination with and celebration of woman as enchantress, as agent of the marvelous, and catalyst of mystical transformation.

Fewer and less significant parallels exist between Ballard's writing and literary surrealism. The author does allude on occasion to Lautréamont and to Rimbaud, and has on one occasion imitated the form of a short piece by Alfred Jarry, who may be considered a proto-surrealist, but I detect no other evidence expressive of inspiration from the poets and writers associated with the surrealist movement. Perhaps ultimately Ballard's most vital and immediate affinity with surrrealism is the applicability to his work of André Breton's doctrine concerning the existence of a transcendent *point sublime*, a state of consciousness "from which life and death, the real and the imaginary, the past and the future, the communicable and the incommunicable, the high and the low, are no longer seen as contradictory."[5] Breton's *point sublime* and Ballard's ontological Eden may be seen as sharing a common non-temporal and non-spatial character, as constituting a condition of consciousness beyond all antinomy, and as representing a state of ultimate awareness and of absolute freedom.

The closest and most profound affinity of Ballard's work is, however, with myth and archetype, with those images and patterns expressive of primordial energies and the deeper life of the psyche. In a sense, myth is both the mode and the meaning of Ballard's writing, constituting both its chief source of imagery and motifs and the very form of conceptualization and manner of consciousness that the work seeks to embody and to impart.

Ballard's oeuvre is informed by archetypal patterns including those of the initiation or rite of passage, the quest for identity, the quest for transcendence, Paradise, the Fall, the underworld or infernal regions, the figure of the savior, the figure of the fertility deity, the figures of the guide or ally and of the antagonist or personification of death, the individuation process including encounters with shadow and anima figures, the process of purgation and self-immolation, the end-of-the-world or apocalypse myth, and the myth of universal regeneration; together with archetypal images such as those of the journey, the sacred marriage or mystical union, light, flight or ascension, water, and the desert or wasteland. The author also employs certain biblical and literary "myths," such as the story of Noah, the fable of Ahasuerus, *The Tempest*, and "The Rime of the Ancient Mariner," for example, to represent primal truths and psychic processes.

The function of myth and archetype in Ballard's writing can be said to be twofold in nature: to enact for the reader in symbolic form the rituals of heroic and mystical initiation, and to awaken in the reader the mythic sensibility, the powers of the visionary imagination. In this manner we are provoked to confront the sense of alienation, the anxieties and inner conflicts that beset us as individuals; and stimulated to struggle against the situations and conditions generated by the larger crisis of our culture, to oppose its staticity and sterility, its estrangement from nature and from the sacred, its essential misapprehensions and its misdirected energies.

J. G. Ballard's contribution to the life of our times has been to extend and to renew what we may call the visionary tradition, to create—out of elements of Romantic literature, surrealism, science fiction, myth, and archetype—a new synthesis expressed in a new idiom, and to invest the visionary tradition with new clarity and new urgency. Through the perceptions and intuitions of his unorthodox sensibility and the creative power of his imagination, Ballard achieves in his work that most essential and most valuable quality of art, which is to provide us with new insights into and new perspectives upon our world, ourselves, and the nature of our being.

Notes

INTRODUCTION

1. See, for example: Anon., "Future Indefinite," in TLS, (August 2, 1963): 593; Peter Nicholls, "Jerry Cornelius at the Atrocity Exhibition: Anarchy and Entropy in *New Worlds Science Fiction* 1964–1974," in *Foundation*, no. 9 (November 1975): 22–44; Derek Mahon, "Crash," in *New Statesman*, no. 92 (December 3 1976): 812–13; Tom Hutchinson, "Blasts of Power," in *Times* (October 1, 1977): 9; Michel Wood, "This is Not the End of the World," in *New York Review of Books* 25, nos. 21–22 (January 25, 1979): 28–31; Patrick Parrinder, *Science Fiction: A Critical Guide* (London: Longman, 1979), 82–83; Paul Ableman, "Desert Song," in *Spectator* (May 30, 1981): 25; Colin Greenland, *The Entropy Exhibition* (London: Routledge, 1983), 92–120; Christopher Lasch, *The Minimal Self* (New York and London: Norton, 1984), 137–41.

2. David Pringle, *Earth Is the Alien Planet: J. G. Ballard's Four Dimensional Nightmare* (San Bernardino: Borgo, 1979).

3. Peter Brigg, *J. G. Ballard* (Mercer Island: Starmont, 1985).

4. Mircea Eliade, *Myths, Dreams and Mysteries* (New York: Harper & Row, 1975), 67.

5. Eliade, *Myths*, 106–7.

6. Joseph Campbell, *The Hero with a Thousand Faces* (New York: Meridian, 1956).

7. Campbell, *Hero*, 243.

8. Northrop Frye, *Anatomy of Criticism* (Princeton: Princeton University Press, 1957).

9. Frye, *Anatomy*, 187–88.

10. Frye, *Anatomy*, 203.

11. M. L. von Franz, "The Process of Individuation," in *Man and His Symbols*, Carl G. Jung, ed. (New York: Dell, 1968), 164.

12. Frieda Fordham, *An Introduction to Jung's Psychology* (London: Penguin, 1968), 49.

13. Franz, "Process," 175.

14. Franz, "Process," 193.

15. R. D. Laing, *The Politics of Experience* (New York: Pantheon, 1967).

16. Aldous Huxley, *The Doors of Perception* (London: Chatto & Windus, 1954).

17. Aldous Huxley, *Heaven and Hell* (London: Chatto & Windus, 1956).

18. Laing, *Politics*, 96.

19. Laing, *Politics*, 99.

20. Laing, *Politics*, 96.

21. Laing, *Politics*, 93.

22. Laing, *Politics*, 97.

23. Huxley, *Doors*, 16.

24. Aldous Huxley, "Knowledge and Understanding" in *Collected Essays* (New York: Harper & Brothers, 1958), 396.

25. Huxley, "Drugs that Shape Men's Minds" in *Collected Essays*, 338.

26. *Re/Search*, no. 8/9 (1984; J. G. Ballard issue): 116.

CHAPTER 1: THE DIMENSION OF THE DISASTER

1. J. G. Ballard, "The Violent Noon," in *Varsity* (Cambridge University student newspaper) (May 26, 1951): 9.

2. J. G. Ballard, "Escapement," *New Worlds* 18, no. 54 (December 1956): 27–39. Collected in *The Venus Hunters*.

3. J. G. Ballard, "Build-Up," *New Worlds* 19, no. 55 (January 1957): 52–70. Re-titled "The Concentration City" in *The Disaster Area*.

4. J. G. Ballard, "Chronopolis," in *New Worlds* 32, no. 92 (March 1960): 64–87. Further parenthetical references are to *Chronopolis* (New York: Berkley, 1971).

5. J. G. Ballard, "Mr. F is Mr. F," in *Science Fantasy* 16, no. 48 (August 1961): 39–56. Further parenthetical references are to *The Disaster Area* (London: Triad/Panther, 1979).

6. J. G. Ballard, "Time of Passage," in *Science Fantasy* 21, no. 63 (February 1964): 85–96. Collected in *The Venus Hunters*.

7. J. G. Ballard, "The Gentle Assassin," in *New Worlds* 38, no. 113 (December 1961): 29–40. Collected in *The Day of Forever*.

8. J. G. Ballard, "Prisoner of the Coral Deep," in *New Worlds* 48, no. 150 (May 1965): 82–88. Further parenthetical references are to *The Day of Forever* (London: Panther, 1985).

9. J. G. Ballard, "The Lost Leonardo," in *Fantasy and Science Fiction* 26, no. 3 (March 1964): 112–28. Further parenthetical references are to *The Terminal Beach* (London: Dent, 1984).

10. J. G. Ballard, "Now Zero," in *Science Fantasy* 13, no. 38 (December 1959): 61–73. Collected in *The Venus Hunters*.

11. J. G. Ballard, "The Man on the 99th Floor," in *New Worlds* 40, no. 120 (July 1962): 36–43. Collected in *The Venus Hunters*.

12. J. G. Ballard, "A Question of Re-entry," in *Fantastic Stories* 12, no. 3 (March 1963): 46–77. Further parenthetical references are to *The Terminal Beach* (London: Dent, 1984).

13. J. G. Ballard, "The Sound Sweep," in *Science Fantasy* 13, no. 39 (February 1960): 2–39. Further parenthetical references are to *The Voices of Time* (London: Dent, 1984).

14. J. G. Ballard, "The Singing Statues," in *Fantastic Stories* 11, no. 7 (July 1962): 6–18. Further parenthetical references are to *Vermillion Sands* (London: Dent, 1985).

15. J. G. Ballard, "Thirteen to Centaurus," in *Amazing Stories* 36, no. 4 (April 1962): 24–47. Further parenthetical references are to *Passport to Eternity* (New York: Berkley, 1963).

16. J. G. Ballard, "The Watch Towers," in *Science Fantasy* 18, no. 53 (June 1962): 51–78. Collected in *Passport to Eternity*.

17. J. G. Ballard, "End Game," in *New Worlds* 44, no. 131 (June 1963): 31–51. Collected in *The Terminal Beach*.

18. J. G. Ballard, "Minus One," in *Science Fantasy* 20, no. 59 (June 1963): 75–86. Further parenthetical references are to *The Disaster Area* (London: Triad/Panther, 1979).

19. J. G. Ballard, "The Waiting Grounds," in *New Worlds* 30, no. 88 (November 1959): 41–69. Further parenthetical references are to *The Day of Forever* (London: Granada, 1985).

20. J. G. Ballard, "The Voices of Time," in *New Worlds* 33, no. 99 (October 1960): 91–123. Further parenthetical references are to *The Voices of Time* (London: Dent, 1984).

21. J. G. Ballard, "The Overloaded Man," in *New Worlds* 36, no. 108 (July 1961): 28–40. Further parenthetical references are to *The Voices of Time* (London: Dent, 1984).

22. J. G. Ballard, "The Garden of Time," in *Fantasy and Science Fiction* 22, no. 2 (February 1962): 5–12. Collected in *Chronopolis*.

23. J. G. Ballard, "The Time Tombs," in *Worlds of If* 13, no. 1 (March 1963): 6–21. Further parenthetical references are to *The Venus Hunters* (London: Granada, 1985).

24. J. G. Ballard, "The Terminal Beach," in *New Worlds* 47, no. 140 (March 1964): 4–24. Further parenthetical references are to *The Terminal Beach* (London: Dent, 1984).

25. J. G. Ballard, "The Delta at Sunset," in *The Terminal Beach* (London: Victor Gollancz, 1964). Further parenthetical references are to *The Terminal Beach* (London: Dent, 1984).

26. J. G. Ballard, "Manhole 69," in *New Worlds* 22, no. 65 (November 1957): 45–67. Further parenthetical references are to *The Disaster Area* (London: Triad/Panther, 1979).

27. J. G. Ballard, "The Thousand Dreams of Stellavista," in *Amazing Stories* 36, no. 3 (March 1962): 48–68. Collected in *Vermillion Sands*.

28. J. G. Ballard, "Now Wakes the Sea," in *Fantasy and Science Fiction* 25, no. 5 (May 1963): 76–85. Collected in *The Disaster Area*.

29. J. G. Ballard, "The Reptile Enclosure" (Original title: "The Sherrington Theory"), in *Amazing Stories* 37, no. 3 (March 1963): 102–13. Further parenthetical references are to *The Terminal Beach* (London: Dent, 1984).

30. J. G. Ballard, "The Gioconda of the Twilight Noon," in *The Terminal Beach* (London: Victor Gollancz, 1964). Further parenthetical references are to *The Terminal Beach* (London: Dent, 1984).

31. J. G. Ballard, "The Venus Hunters" (Original title: "The Encounter"), in *Amazing Stories* 37, no. 6 (June 1963): 88–118. Further parenthetical references are to *The Venus Hunters* (London: Granada, 1985).

32. J. G. Ballard, "The Drowned Giant" (Original title: "Souvenir"), in *Playboy* 12, no. 5 (May 1965): 98, 108, 192–95. Further parenthetical references are to *The Terminal Beach* (London: Dent, 1984).

33. J. G. Ballard, "Track 12," in *New Worlds* 24, no. 70 (April 1958): 62–67. Collected in *The Venus Hunters*.

34. J. G. Ballard, "The Man on the 99th Floor," in *New Worlds* 40, no. 120 (July 1962): 36–43. Collected in *The Day of Forever*.

35. J. G. Ballard, "Studio 5, the Stars," in *Science Fantasy* 15, no. 45 (February 1961): 69–103. Collected in *Vermillion Sands*.

36. J. G. Ballard, "Passport to Eternity," in *Amazing Stories* 36, no. 6 (June 1962): 56–74. Collected in *Passport to Eternity*.

37. J. G. Ballard, "Billenium," in *New Worlds* 38, no. 112 (November 1961): 43–58. Collected in *The Terminal Beach*.

38. J. G. Ballard, "The Insane Ones," in *Amazing Stories* 36, no. 1 (January 1962): 36–46. Further parenthetical references are to *The Day of Forever* (London: Granada, 1985).

39. J. G. Ballard, "The Subliminal Man," in *New Worlds* 42, no. 126 (January 1963): 109–26. Further parenthetical references are to *The Disaster Area* (London: Triad/Panther, 1979).

40. J. G. Ballard, "Zone of Terror," in *New Worlds* 32, no. 95 (March 1960): 52–69. Further parenthetical references are to *The Disaster Area* (London: Triad/Panther, 1979).

41. J. G. Ballard, "Deep End," in *New Worlds* 36, no. 106 (May 1961): 111–22. Further parenthetical references are to *The Terminal Beach* (London: Dent, 1984).

CHAPTER 2: A CATECHISM OF CATACLYSM

1. J. G. Ballard, "Introduction to Cataclysms and Dooms," in *The Visual Encyclopedia of Science Fiction*, Brian Ash, ed., (London: Trewin Copplestone Publishing, 1977): 130.

2. J. G. Ballard, *The Wind from Nowhere* (New York: Berkley, 1962). Further parenthetical references are to this edition.

3. J. G. Ballard, *The Drowned World* (New York: Berkley, 1962). Further parenthetical references are to *The Drowned World* (London: Dent, 1983).

4. J. G. Ballard, *The Drought* (Harmondsworth: Penguin, 1968). Original title: *The Burning World* (New York: Berkley, 1964). *The Drought* is the revised, definitive edition of the novel. Further parenthetical references are to *The Drought* (London: Panther/Triad, 1978).

5. J. G. Ballard, *The Crystal World* (London: Jonathan Cape, 1966). Further parenthetical references are to *The Crystal World* (New York: Berkley, 1967).

6. The interested reader is referred to the discussion of luminosity and precious stones as characteristic of paradises and other worlds in Aldous Huxley's *Heaven and Hell* (London: Chatto & Windus, 1956).

CHAPTER 3: TECHNOLOGICAL TARTARUS

1. J. G. Ballard, *The Atrocity Exhibition* (London: Jonathan Cape, 1970). Further parenthetical references are to *The Atrocity Exhibition* (London: Triad/Granada, 1985).

2. J. G. Ballard, *Crash* (London: Jonathan Cape, 1973). Further parenthetical references are to *Crash* (London: Triad/Granada, 1985).

3. Graeme Revell, "J. G. Ballard interviewed by Graeme Revell," in *Re/Search* no. 8/9 (1984): 47.

4. J. G. Ballard, *Concrete Island* (London: Jonathan Cape, 1974). Further parenthetical references are to *Concrete Island* (London: Triad/Granada, 1985).

5. J. G. Ballard, *High Rise* (London: Jonathan Cape, 1975). Further parenthetical references are to *High Rise* (London: Triad/Granada, 1985).

CHAPTER 4: "TRAPPED AIRCRAFT"

1. J. G. Ballard, "Tomorrow is a Million Years," in *New Worlds* 50, no. 171 (March 1967): 119–21. Further parenthetical references are to *The Day of Forever* (London: Granada, 1985).

2. J. G. Ballard, "Cry Hope, Cry Fury," in *Fantasy and Science Fiction* 33, no. 4 (October 1967): 114–28. Further parenthetical references are to *Vermillion Sands* (London: Dent, 1985).

3. J. G. Ballard, "The Dead Astronaut," in *Playboy* (May 1968): 118–20, 116–68. Collected in *Low-Flying Aircraft.*

4. J. G. Ballard, "Say Goodbye to the Wind," in *Fantastic Stories* 19, no. 8 (August 1970): 36– 45, 134. Further parenthetical references are to *Vermillion Sands* (London: Dent, 1985).

5. J. G. Ballard, "The Beach Murders," in *New Worlds*, no. 189 (April 1969): 27–31. Collected in *Low-Flying Aircraft.*

6. J. G. Ballard, "The Smile," in *Bananas*, no. 6 (Autumn-Winter 1976): 8–10. Further parenthetical references are to *Myths of the Near Future* (London: Triad/Granada, 1984).

7. J. G. Ballard, "Having a Wonderful Time," in *Bananas*, no. 10 (Spring 1978): 24–30. Further parenthetical references are to *Myths of the Near Future* (London: Triad/Granada, 1984).

8. J. G. Ballard, "The Secret History of World War III," in *Ambit*, 114, (Autumn 1988); reprinted in *The Orbit Science Fiction Yearbook Two*, David S. Garnett, ed., (London: Futura, 1989): 17–27.

9. J. G. Ballard, "War Fever," *Fantasy and Science Fiction* 77, no. 4 (October 1989): 92–111.

10. J. G. Ballard, "The Impossible Man," in *The Impossible Man and Other Stories* (New York: Berkley, 1966). Further parenthetical references are to *The Disaster Area* (London: Triad/Panther, 1979).

11. J. G. Ballard, "The 60 Minute Zoom," in *Bananas*, no. 5 (Summer 1976): 18–20. Further parenthetical references are to *The Venus Hunters* (London: Granada, 1985).

12. J. G. Ballard, "The Killing Ground," in *New Worlds*, no. 188 (March 1969): 47–50. Further parenthetical references are to *The Venus Hunters* (London: Granada, 1985).

13. J. G. Ballard, "Theatre of War," in *Bananas*, no. 9 (Winter 1977): 21–25. Collected in *Myths of the Near Future.*

14. J. G. Ballard, "The Greatest Television Show on Earth," in *Ambit*, no. 53 (Winter 1972–73): 29–32. Further parenthetical references are to *Low-Flying Aircraft* (London: Triad/Granada, 1985).

15. J. G. Ballard, "The Life and Death of God," in *Ambit*, no. 66 (Spring 1976): 5–10. Further parenthetical references are to *Low-Flying Aircraft* (London: Triad/Granada, 1985).

16. J. G. Ballard, "The Intensive Care Unit," in *Ambit*, no. 71 (Summer 1977): 3–9. Further parenthetical references are to *Myths of the Near Future* (London: Triad/Granada, 1984).

17. J. G. Ballard, "Motel Architecture," in *Bananas*, no. 12 (Autumn 1978): 34–7. Further parenthetical references are to *Myths of the Near Future* (London: Triad/Granada, 1984).

18. J. G. Ballard, "A Host of Furious Fancies," in *Time Out* (19 December 1980): 34–37. Further parenthetical references are to *Myths of the Near Future* (London: Triad/Granada, 1984).

19. J. G. Ballard, "The Object of the Attack," in *Interzone*, no. 9 (Autumn 1984): 4–10.

20. J. G. Ballard, "The Day of Forever," in *The Impossible Man and Other Stories* (New York: Berkley, 1966). Further parenthetical references are to *The Day of Forever* (London: Granada, 1985).

21. J. G. Ballard, "Storm Bird, Storm Dreamer," in *New Worlds* 50, no. 168 (November 1966): 4–25. Further parenthetical references are to *The Disaster Area* (London: Triad/Panther, 1979).

22. J. G. Ballard, "Journey Across a Crater," in *New Worlds*, no. 198 (February 1970): 2–5.

23. J. G. Ballard, "My Dream of Flying to Wake Island," in *Ambit*, no. 60 (Autumn 1974): 60–66. Further parenthetical references are to *Low-Flying Aircraft* (London: Triad/Granada, 1985).

24. J. G. Ballard, "Low-Flying Aircraft," in *Bananas*, no. 2 (Summer 1975): 6–9. Further parenthetical references are to *Low-Flying Aircraft* (London: Triad/Granada, 1985).

25. J. G. Ballard, "The Ultimate City," in *Low-Flying Aircraft* (London: Jonathan Cape, 1976). Further parenthetical references are to *Low-Flying Aircraft* (London: Triad/Granada, 1985).

26. J. G. Ballard, "Notes Toward a Mental Breakdown," in *Re/Search*, nos. 8/9 (1984): 76–79.

27. J. G. Ballard, "Zodiac 2000," in *Ambit*, no. 75 (Summer 1978): 4–10. Further parenthetical references are to *Myths of the Near Future* (London: Triad/Granada, 1984).

28. J. G. Ballard, "News from the Sun," in *Ambit*, no. 87 (Autumn 1981): 2–28. Further parenthetical references are to *Myths of the Near Future* (London: Triad/Granada, 1984).

29. J. G. Ballard, "Memories of the Space Age," in *Interzone* 1, no. 2 (Summer 1982): 3–13.

30. J. G. Ballard, "Myths of the Near Future," in *Fantasy and Science Fiction* 62, no. 4 (October 1982): 50–76. Further parenthetical references are to *Myths of the Near Future* (London: Triad/Granada, 1984).

31. J. G. Ballard, "The Man Who Walked on the Moon," in *Interzone* 1, no. 13 (Autumn 1985): 3–9. Further parenthetical references are to *Interzone: The 2nd Anthology*, John Clute, David Pringle, and Simon Ounsley, eds. (New York: St. Martin's Press, 1987).

CHAPTER 5: RELEASE

1. J. G. Ballard, *The Unlimited Dream Company* (London: Jonathan Cape, 1979). Further parenthetical references are to this edition.

2. J. G. Ballard, *Hello America* (London: Jonathan Cape, 1981). Further parenthetical references are to this edition.

3. J. G. Ballard, *Empire of the Sun* (London: Victor Gollancz, 1984). Further parenthetical references are to this edition.

4. J. G. Ballard, *The Day of Creation* (London: Victor Gollancz, 1987). Further parenthetical references are to this edition.

5. J. G. Ballard, *Running Wild* (London: Century Hutchinson, 1988). Further parenthetical references are to this edition.

CONCLUSION

1. Judith Merril, "Books," in *Fantasy and Science Fiction* 30, no. 1 (January 1966): 51.

2. William S. Burroughs, "Preface to *Love and Napalm: Export U.S.A.*," in J. G. Ballard, *Love and Napalm: Export U.S.A.* (New York: Grove Press, 1972). The title of this book in its original U.K. edition is *The Atrocity Exhibition*.

3. J. G. Ballard, "Which Way to Inner Space?" in *New Worlds* 40, no. 118 (May 1962): 2–3, 116–18. Further parenthetical references are to this source.

4. J. G. Ballard, "The Coming of the Unconscious," in *New Worlds* 50, no. 164 (July 1966): 141–146.

5. André Breton, *Manifestes du Surréalisme* (Paris: Jean Jacques Pauvert, 1962): 154.

Selected Bibliography

The following bibliography is not intended to be comprehensive: indeed, it could not be so without constituting a volume in itself. The reader will find all of Ballard's novels listed below, as well as those collections of short fiction which together contain very nearly all of the author's short stories published to date. Certain earlier collections, which are no longer in print, and later compilations of short fiction have been omitted, together with those stories which as yet remain uncollected. Most of these latter are listed in my notes. Of Ballard's essays I have included only those I consider to be the most essential. Likewise, my selection of criticism of Ballard's work is restricted to those reviews or articles which seem to me to be the most acute and substantial. The definitive listing of primary and secondary literature of J. G. Ballard is David Pringle's bibliography, which I have included among the entries below. I recommend it to every serious Ballard scholar, collector or enthusiast.

SELECTED WORKS BY J. G. BALLARD

Novels

The Drowned World. New York: Berkley, 1962.
The Wind from Nowhere. New York: Berkley, 1962.
The Drought. London: Jonathan Cape, 1965.
The Crystal World. London: Jonathan Cape, 1966.
Crash. London: Jonathan Cape, 1973.
Concrete Island. London: Jonathan Cape, 1974.
High-Rise. London: Jonathan Cape, 1975.
The Unlimited Dream Company. London: Jonathan Cape, 1979.
Hello America. London: Jonathan Cape, 1981.
Empire of the Sun. London: Victor Gollancz, 1984.

The Day of Creation. London: Victor Gollancz, 1987.
Running Wild. London: Century Hutchinson, 1988.

Collections of Short Fiction

Billenium. New York: Berkley, 1962.
The Voices of Time. New York: Berkley, 1962.
The Four-Dimensional Nightmare. London: Victor Gollancz, 1963.
Passport to Eternity. New York, Berkley, 1963.
The Terminal Beach. New York, Berkley, 1964.
The Terminal Beach. London: Victor Gollancz, 1964. (Contents differ considerably from those of Berkley edition.)
The Day of Forever. London: Panther Books, 1966.
The Impossible Man. New York: Berkley, 1966.
The Disaster Area. London: Jonathan Cape, 1967.
The Overloaded Man. London: Panther Books, 1967.
The Atrocity Exhibition. London: Jonathan Cape, 1970.
Chronopolis. New York: Putnam, 1971.
Vermillion Sands. New York: Putnam, 1971.
Low-Flying Aircraft. London: Jonathan Cape, 1976.
The Venus Hunters. London: Granada, 1980.
Myths of the Near Future. London: Jonathan Cape, 1982.

Nonfiction

"Which Way to Inner Space?" *New Worlds* 40, no. 118 (May 1962): 2–3, 116–18.
"The Coming of the Unconscious." *New Worlds* 50, no. 164 (July 1966): 141–46.
"Notes from Nowhere: Comments on Work in Progress." *New Worlds* 50, no. 167 (October 1966): 147–51.
"Introduction to Cataclysms and Dooms." In *The Visual Encyclopedia of Science Fiction*, edited by Brian Ash, 130. London: Trewin Copplestone Publishing, 1978.

SELECTED INTERVIEWS WITH J. G. BALLARD

MacBeth, George. "The New Science Fiction: A Conversation between J. G. Ballard and George MacBeth." In *The New SF*, edited by Langdon Jones, 52–60. London: Hutchinson, 1969.
Reed, Douglas. "Ballard at Home." *Books and Bookmen* (April 1972: 11–12, 41.
Evan, Chris. "The Space Age Is Over." *Penthouse* 14 (April 1979): 39–42, 102, 106.

Platt, Charles. "J. G. Ballard." In *Dream Makers: The Uncommon People Who Write Science Fiction*, 215–25. New York: Berkley, 1980.

Burns, Alan and Charles Sugnet. "J. G. Ballard." In *The Imagination on Trial: British and American Writers Discuss Their Working Methods*, 15–30. London & New York: Alison & Busby, 1981.

Pringle, David. "The Profession of Science Fiction, 26: From Shanghai to Shepperton." *Foundation: The Review of Science Fiction*, no. 24 (February 1982): 5–23.

Frick, Thomas. "The Art of Fiction LXXXV: J. G. Ballard." *Paris Review* 94 (Winter 1984): 132–60.

Juno, A. and Vale. "Interview with JGB." *Re/Search*, nos. 8/9 (1984): 6–35.

Revell, Graeme. "Interview with JGB." *Re/Search*, nos. 8/9 (1984): 42–52.

Pringle, David. "Psychoanalyst of the Electronic Age." *Words: The New Literary Forum* 1, no. 4 (September 1985): 24–27.

Verniere, James. "A Conversation with J. G. Ballard." *Twilight Zone* 8, no. 2 (June 1988): 46–50, 89.

Pringle, David. "Memoirs for a Space Age." *Fear* 14 (February 1990): 26–27; *Fear* 15 (March 1990): 26–27.

SELECTED CRITICISM OF J. G. BALLARD

Books

Pringle, David. *Earth is the Alien Planet: J. G. Ballard's Four-Dimensional Nightmare*. San Bernardino: Borgo Press, 1974.

Goddard, James and David Pringle, eds. *J. G. Ballard: The First Twenty Years*. Hayes, Middlesex: Bran's Head Books, 1976.

Greenland, Colin. "The Works of J. G. Ballard." Chapter 7 in *The Entropy Exhibition: Michael Moorcock and the British "New Wave" in Science Fiction*, 92–120. London: Routledge, 1983.

Brigg, Peter. *J. G. Ballard*. Mercer Island, Washington: Starmont House, 1985.

Articles and Reviews

Merril, Judith. "Books." *Fantasy and Science Fiction* 30, no. 1 (January 1966): 51–59.

———. "Books." *Fantasy and Science Fiction* 31, no. 2 (August 1966): 57–69.

Moorcock, Michael. "Ballard: The Voice." *New Worlds* 50, no. 167 (October 1966): 2–3, 151.

Ryan, Anthony. "The Mind of Mr. J. G. Ballard." *Foundation: The Review of Science Fiction*, no. 3 (March 1973): 44–48.

Perry, Nick and Roy Wilkie. "The Undivided Self: J. G. Ballard's *The Crystal World*." *Riverside Quarterly* 5, no. 4 (April 1973): 268–77.

Pringle, David. "The Fourfold Symbolism of J. G. Ballard." *Foundation: The Review of Science Fiction*, no. 4 (July 1973): 48–60.

Durrant, Digby. "Squibs and Rockets: A Note on J. G. Ballard." *London Magazine* 15, no. 5 (December 1975/January 1976): 69–73.

Nicol, Charles. "J. G. Ballard and the Limits of Mainstream SF." *Science Fiction Studies* 3, no. 2 (July 1976): 150–57.

Rathbone, Julian. "The Ultimate Work." *The Literary Review* 2, no. 39 (August 1981): 8–10.

BIBLIOGRAPHIES OF J. G. BALLARD

Goddard, James. *J. G. Ballard: A Bibliography*. Milford on Sea, Hampshire: Cypher Press, 1970.

Pringle, David. *J. G. Ballard: A Primary and Secondary Bibliography*. Boston: G. K. Hall, 1984.

Index

About the Author

GREGORY STEPHENSON is a Lecturer at Roskilde University, Roskilde, Denmark. An American, he specializes in American and British literature of the nineteenth and twentieth centuries. He has published widely on Ballard and other contemporary writers, and his particular interest in "The Beats" is reflected in books such as *The Daybreak Boys: Essays on the Literature of the Beat Generation*. Stephenson is also publisher and editor of *Pearl*, a literary journal.